Professional Networking

Building Connections for Success

JOSEPH KENDRICK

TABLE OF CONTENTS

Introduction

1. Introduction to Professional Networking
    1.1 Understanding the Importance of Networking
    1.2 Benefits and Advantages of Building Professional Connections

2. The Foundations of Effective Networking
    2.1 Developing a Networking Mindset
    2.2 Setting Networking Goals
    2.3 Identifying Target Connections

3. Building and Maintaining a Professional Network
    3.1 Creating a Powerful Personal Brand
    3.2 Leveraging Social Media for Networking
    3.3 Attending Networking Events and Conferences
3.4 Joining Professional Associations and Organizations
3.5 Nurturing Relationships Through Effective Communication
    3.6 Building a Network of Mentors and Advisors

4. Networking Strategies for Different Scenarios
    4.1 Networking within the Workplace
    4.2 Networking for Career Advancement

4.3 Networking as an Entrepreneur or Small Business Owner

4.4 Networking for Job Seekers and Career Changers

4.5 Networking in the Digital Age: Online Platforms and Virtual Connections

5. Overcoming Networking Challenges and Obstacles

5.1 Overcoming Fear and Shyness in Networking

5.2 Building Authentic Connections

5.3 Managing Time and Prioritising Network Building Activities

5.4 Dealing with Rejection and Overcoming Setbacks

6. Enhancing Networking Skills

6.1 Effective and Engaging Conversation Techniques

6.2 Developing Active Listening Skills

6.3 Establishing and Maintaining Rapport

6.4 Mastering the Art of Follow-up and Relationship Building

7. Cultivating a Network of Resources

7.1 Building a Network of Industry Experts and Thought Leaders

7.2 Establishing Collaborative Partnerships

7.3 Leveraging Your Network for Professional Opportunities

7.4 Creating a Supportive Network for Personal and Professional Growth

8. Networking Etiquette and Best Practices

8.1 Understanding Professional Networking Etiquette

8.2 Networking Do's and Don'ts

8.3 Effective Networking Communication: In Person and Online

8.4 Networking for Diversity and Inclusion

9. Harnessing the Power of Networking for Success

9.1 Using Your Network to Access Opportunities

9.2 Leveraging Referrals and Recommendations

9.3 Building a Reputation as a Connector and Influencer

10. Networking for Long-Term Success

10.1 Maintaining and Sustaining Professional Relationships

10.2 Embracing Lifelong Learning and Continuous Networking

10.3 Expanding and Diversifying Your Network

10.4 Paying It Forward: Becoming a Networking Mentor

11. Conclusion: The Power of Networking in Achieving Success

INTRODUCTION

In today's fast-paced and interconnected world, building professional connections has become more important than ever. Whether you're seeking career advancement, exploring new opportunities, or simply looking to expand your knowledge and resources, a strong professional network can be a powerful asset.

This book, "Professional Networking: Building Connections for Success," is designed to provide you with the knowledge, strategies, and skills necessary to develop and maintain a robust network that will propel you towards your goals.

In this introductory section, we will explore the importance of networking and the numerous benefits it brings. We will delve into the foundations of effective networking, including developing the right mindset, setting goals, and identifying target connections.

From there, we will guide you through the process of building and nurturing your professional network. You will learn how to create a powerful personal brand, leverage the power of social media, attend networking events and conferences, join relevant associations and organisations, and effectively communicate and maintain relationships. We will also discuss the importance of establishing a network of mentors and advisors who can provide valuable guidance and support along your professional journey.

This book goes beyond the basics and provides networking strategies for various scenarios, such as networking within the workplace, advancing your career, navigating entrepreneurship, and seeking new job opportunities. We will also explore the impact of the digital age on networking, including online platforms and virtual connections.

Networking can present its own set of challenges, such as fear and shyness, building authentic connections, managing time effectively, and facing rejection. In this book, we will address these obstacles head-on and provide practical tips and techniques for overcoming them.

Enhancing your networking skills is crucial for success, and we have dedicated an entire section to it. We will discuss effective conversation techniques, active listening skills, establishing rapport, and mastering the art of follow-up and relationship-building.

Cultivating a network of resources is another essential aspect of professional networking. We will explore how to connect with industry experts and thought leaders, establish collaborative partnerships, leverage your network for opportunities, and create a supportive environment for personal and professional growth.

Networking etiquette and best practices will also be covered extensively. Understanding professional networking etiquette, following networking do's and don'ts, and effectively communicating in person and online are key to making meaningful connections. We will also discuss the importance of networking for diversity and inclusion.

Throughout this book, we emphasise the power of networking in achieving success. You will learn how to use your network to access opportunities, leverage referrals and recommendations, and ultimately build a reputation as a connector and influencer.

Networking isn't a one-time endeavour; it's a lifelong journey. In the final sections, we will explore how to maintain and sustain professional relationships, embrace lifelong learning and continuous networking, expand and diversify your network, and pay it forward by becoming a networking mentor.

By the time you reach the conclusion, you will have gained a comprehensive understanding of professional networking and the tools and strategies needed to build and leverage a network for long-term success. Get ready to unlock the power of networking and propel yourself towards the achievements and opportunities you deserve.

CHAPTER 1

Introduction to Professional Networking

Professional networking refers to the practice of establishing and nurturing professional relationships with individuals who can help further your career or business objectives. It involves connecting with people in your industry or field of interest, and building mutually beneficial relationships by exchanging knowledge, support, and opportunities.

Professional networking can be done in person or online, and it typically involves attending networking events, joining industry associations or groups, and utilising professional social media platforms. The goal of professional networking is to expand your network of contacts, gain access to new opportunities, and build a strong professional reputation.

Benefits of professional networking include:

1. Access to opportunities: Networking provides a platform to learn about job openings, business partnerships, or collaboration opportunities that might not be publicly advertised.

2. Knowledge sharing: By connecting with professionals in your field, you can exchange ideas, expertise, and industry insights, enabling you to stay updated with the latest trends and developments.

3. Career advancement: Networking can open doors to mentorship, career advice, and potential referrals for job opportunities or promotions.

4. Increased visibility and credibility: Building strong relationships with professionals in your industry can help establish your reputation, making you a trusted resource or thought leader.

5. Support system: Networking allows you to connect with like-minded individuals who can offer support, guidance, and encouragement throughout your career journey.

Tips for effective professional networking include:

1. Be proactive: Take initiative by reaching out to professionals in your industry. Attend events, join relevant groups, and engage in conversations both online and offline.

2. Build genuine relationships: Networking is about building meaningful connections, so be authentic and show a genuine interest in others. Focus on building relationships rather than just asking for favours.

3. Offer value: Find ways to provide value to your network by sharing knowledge, resources, or connections. A helpful and generous approach will enhance your reputation and foster stronger relationships.

4. Follow up and stay connected: After meeting someone, make sure to follow up with a personalised thank-you note and stay connected over time. Regularly reach out to your network to maintain relationships and show your continued interest and support.

5. Be patient and persistent: Networking is a long-term investment, and it takes time to establish and nurture relationships. Be patient and persistent in building your network, as it can pay off in the long run.

Overall, professional networking is a crucial skill for career growth and success. By actively building and maintaining a strong network of contacts, you can enhance your professional opportunities, gain valuable insights, and establish a reputation that sets you apart from others in your field.

Networking is important for several reasons:

1. Access to opportunities: Networking provides access to a larger pool of opportunities, both in terms of job openings and business prospects. Often, the best opportunities are found through personal connections rather than traditional job boards or advertisements. Having a strong network can give you a competitive edge in finding new career or business prospects.

2. Knowledge and insights: By networking with professionals in your field, you have the opportunity to exchange knowledge, insights, and best practices. This can help you stay up to date with industry trends, learn new skills, and gain valuable information that can enhance your professional growth.

3. Career advancement: Networking can play a crucial role in career advancement. By building relationships with influential individuals, mentors, or industry leaders, you can gain valuable guidance and advice on how to progress in your career. These

connections can also provide recommendations or referrals that can open doors to new opportunities.

4. Building your personal brand: Networking allows you to showcase your expertise, skills, and accomplishments to a wider audience. By consistently engaging and adding value to your network, you can establish a strong personal brand and reputation, which can help attract new opportunities and collaborations.

5. Emotional support and motivation: Building a strong professional network provides a support system of like-minded individuals who can understand and empathise with the challenges and successes within your industry. Having a network of peers and mentors can provide emotional support, encouragement, and motivation, especially during challenging times.

6. Increased confidence and self-esteem: Networking helps improve your communication and interpersonal skills, which can boost your confidence and overall professional development. The more you engage with others in a professional setting, the more comfortable and confident you become in presenting yourself, sharing your ideas, and engaging in meaningful conversations.

7. Collaboration and partnerships: Networking allows you to connect with potential collaborators, partners, or clients. By expanding your network, you can find individuals or businesses that complement your skills or services, leading to mutually beneficial partnerships or collaborations.

Networking should be viewed as an ongoing and long-term investment in your professional growth. It requires effort, consistency, and a genuine interest in building meaningful relationships. The benefits of networking can extend beyond immediate opportunities and play a significant role in your long-term career success.

1.1 The Importance of Networking

In today's highly competitive and rapidly evolving professional landscape, the importance of networking cannot be overstated. Gone are the days when success relied solely on individual capabilities and qualifications. In the interconnected world we live in, building and nurturing a strong professional network has become a prerequisite for career advancement and personal growth.

Networking is not just about collecting business cards or adding connections on social media; it is about forging genuine, meaningful relationships with others in your industry or field of interest. It involves building a web of connections that can offer support, guidance, resources, and opportunities.

One of the most evident benefits of networking is the expansion of your knowledge and skill set. By connecting with professionals in different domains and industries, you gain access to a wealth of insights, perspectives, and expertise. This exposure can broaden your horizons, challenge your thinking, and inspire you to explore new avenues and possibilities within your own field.

Another major advantage of networking is the increased visibility and credibility it brings. When you develop a strong reputation within your network as a knowledgeable and reliable professional, others are more likely to turn to you for advice, collaboration, or potential job opportunities. Your network becomes a valuable platform to showcase your skills, achievements, and thought leadership, which can lead to enhanced career prospects and recognition.

In addition, networking provides access to a vast pool of resources and opportunities. Your network can serve as a source of new leads, job openings, partnerships, and industry insights. A referral or recommendation from a trusted contact can carry significant weight and open doors that might otherwise remain closed. By nurturing your network effectively, you increase your chances of finding valuable connections who can provide support, mentorship, or even become collaborators or clients.

Building a solid professional network also fosters personal and professional growth. Networking exposes you to diverse perspectives, challenges and motivates you to continuously improve, and offers opportunities for skill development. The relationships you cultivate can provide valuable feedback, guidance, and accountability, pushing you to strive for excellence and reach your full potential.

Networking provides a platform for collaboration and innovation. By connecting with like-minded professionals who share your passion or vision, you can create partnerships and engage in collaborative projects that have the potential to drive impactful change in your industry. The synergistic power of diverse talents and ideas can lead to breakthroughs, new ventures, and transformative solutions.

Networking helps cultivate a support system that can provide emotional and professional support throughout your career journey. The challenges and setbacks that we inevitably face can be easier to navigate with the support and encouragement of a trusted network. They can offer useful advice, share their own experiences, and provide a sense of camaraderie that helps you push through difficult times.

Networking is an essential aspect of professional success in today's interconnected world. It offers numerous benefits, including expanding knowledge and skills, increasing visibility and credibility, accessing resources and opportunities, fostering personal and professional growth, driving collaboration and innovation, and providing a support system. By recognizing the significance of networking and actively investing in building and nurturing your network, you are equipping yourself with a powerful tool for success in your career endeavours.

1.2 Benefits and Advantages of Building Professional Connections

Building professional connections offers numerous benefits and advantages for individuals in any industry or field. Some of the key benefits include:

1. Access to Opportunities: Building professional connections gives you access to a wider network of individuals who can provide you with job leads, career opportunities, and collaborations. Opportunities often arise through word-of-mouth referrals or introductions from your network.

2. Industry Insights and Knowledge Sharing: Through professional connections, you gain access to a wealth of industry insights, trends, and best practices. Engaging with professionals who have different experiences and perspectives allows you to expand your knowledge base and stay up-to-date with the latest developments in your field.

3. Personal and Professional Growth: Building professional connections provides opportunities for personal and professional growth. Your network can offer guidance, mentorship, and constructive feedback, helping you develop new skills, overcome challenges, and achieve your career goals.

4. Support System and Collaboration: A strong professional network serves as a support system, providing emotional support, advice, and encouragement. Collaboration opportunities with like-minded professionals can arise, leading to joint projects, shared resources, and the ability to tackle complex challenges collectively.

5. Expanded Reach and Visibility: Building professional connections exposes you to a wider audience and increases your visibility within your industry. By attending events, participating in discussions, and sharing your expertise, you become more recognizable and establish yourself as a credible and knowledgeable professional.

6. Access to Resources: Your professional network can provide access to valuable resources, including industry-specific tools, software, research, and training opportunities. Being connected to individuals who have access to these resources can save you time and money in sourcing them independently.

7. Enhanced Confidence and Communication Skills: Networking requires you to interact and engage with professionals from various backgrounds and levels of expertise. Through frequent networking interactions, you can grow your confidence,

improve your communication skills, and develop the ability to make connections with ease.

8. Career Advancement: Building professional connections can lead to career advancement opportunities. Your network can provide recommendations, introduce you to influential individuals, and open doors to job promotions or entrepreneurial ventures.

9. Peer Validation and Support: Connecting with professionals who share similar goals and challenges can provide validation and support. Sharing experiences with like-minded individuals helps you realise that others have faced similar obstacles and can inspire you to overcome them.

10. Long-lasting Relationships: Building professional connections often leads to long-lasting relationships. Your network can become a source of friendship, collaboration, and ongoing support throughout your career journey.

Building professional connections offers a multitude of benefits, ranging from access to opportunities and resources to personal and professional growth. Investing time and effort into networking is essential for career success and can lead to significant career advancements and personal fulfilment.

CHAPTER 2

Foundations of Effective Networking

The foundations of effective networking lie in several key principles and strategies. Here are some foundational elements that can help you build and maintain a strong professional network:

1. Define Your Goals: Before you start networking, it's crucial to define your goals and objectives. Ask yourself what you want to achieve through networking – whether it's career advancement, finding new opportunities, expanding your knowledge, or simply building meaningful relationships. Knowing your goals will help you focus your efforts and make targeted connections.

2. Be Authentic and Genuine: Authenticity is key when it comes to networking. Be genuine in your interactions and show a sincere interest in others. Building trust and rapport is more likely when people perceive your intentions to be genuine and not solely driven by personal gain.

3. Attend Networking Events: Attend relevant industry conferences, seminars, workshops, and other events where you can meet professionals in

your field. These events provide valuable opportunities to connect with like-minded individuals, exchange ideas, and build relationships in a more informal setting.

4. Utilise Social Media: In today's digital era, social media platforms such as LinkedIn, Twitter, and Facebook are powerful tools for networking. Create a professional online presence, engage in industry-specific discussions, and connect with professionals in your field. Social media can help you expand your network beyond geographical boundaries and maintain ongoing connections.

5. Maintain a Two-Way Relationship: Networking is not just about taking; it's about giving as well. Offer your expertise, help others when you can, and be a resource for your network. Building a strong network is about mutual support and collaboration, so be proactive in offering assistance and opportunities to others.

6. Follow Up and Stay in Touch: Following up after initial meetings or interactions is crucial to maintaining and nurturing professional connections. Send a personalised thank-you note or email, connect on social media, and periodically check in. Build a system for staying in touch, whether it's

through regular coffee meetings, virtual catch-ups, or attending industry events together.

7. Network Beyond Your Immediate Circle: While it's important to build connections within your own profession or industry, don't limit yourself to just that. Expand your networking efforts to related industries, complementary fields, and diverse sectors. Embracing diversity in your network will offer fresh perspectives and a broader range of opportunities.

8. Be a Good Listener and Ask Meaningful Questions: Networking is not just about showcasing your achievements and aspirations. Be an active listener, show genuine interest in others' experiences, and ask thoughtful questions. This demonstrates your willingness to learn and build authentic connections.

9. Seek Out Professional Associations and Groups: Joining professional associations, industry-specific organisations, or interest-based groups can provide valuable networking platforms. These communities often offer regular events, educational opportunities, and forums where you can engage with professionals who share common interests.

10. Cultivate a Positive Online Presence: In addition to maintaining meaningful offline connections, pay attention to your online presence. Ensure that your professional profiles and platforms reflect a positive image. Share insightful content, contribute to discussions, and engage with others' posts in a respectful and constructive manner.

Building and maintaining a robust professional network takes time and effort. However, by following these foundational principles, you can establish long-lasting connections, gain access to numerous opportunities, and enhance your personal and professional growth.

2.1 Developing a Networking Mindset

Building an effective professional network starts with developing a networking mindset. It's important to approach networking as an ongoing process rather than a one-time activity. Here are some key elements to consider when developing a networking mindset:

1. Recognize the Value of Networking: Understand the benefits and advantages of networking.

Networking can open doors to new opportunities, provide access to valuable resources and information, and offer support and guidance from like-minded professionals. Recognizing the inherent value of networking will motivate you to invest time and effort into building and maintaining your network.

2. Embrace a Growth Mindset: Adopt a growth mindset, which involves believing in your ability to learn and grow through networking. Approach networking with curiosity and a willingness to explore new perspectives, ideas, and opportunities. Embracing a growth mindset will help you see networking as a continuous learning journey rather than a transactional process.

3. Shift Your Mindset from Taking to Giving: Networking is not solely about what you can gain; it's also about what you can contribute. Shift your mindset from solely focusing on your own needs to genuinely wanting to help others. By being a resource, offering support, and contributing to the success of others, you'll build strong and mutually beneficial relationships.

4. Be Open to Collaboration and Partnership: Networking is not just about building connections for personal gain; it's also about fostering

collaboration and partnership. Embrace an abundance mindset and recognize that by working together, you can achieve more significant outcomes. Be open to collaboration, share your knowledge and expertise, and seek opportunities to support others in their journey.

5. Stay Persistent and Resilient: Building a professional network takes time and effort, and it's important to remain persistent and resilient. Networking involves putting yourself out there, facing rejections, and overcoming setbacks. Adopt a resilient mindset that enables you to bounce back from challenges and continue to cultivate connections.

6. Cultivate a Positive Attitude: A positive attitude can greatly impact your networking efforts. Approach networking with enthusiasm, optimism, and a genuine desire to connect with others. Positivity is contagious and can help build rapport, attract like-minded individuals, and foster meaningful professional relationships.

7. Practise Active Networking: Networking shouldn't be confined to specific events or occasions. Develop a mindset of active networking by consistently seeking opportunities to connect with professionals in your field. Be proactive in

reaching out, engaging with others, and staying updated on industry trends and developments. Actively engaging in networking activities will help you build a strong and dynamic professional network.

By developing a networking mindset and embracing the principles of networking, you can lay a solid foundation for building and maintaining a robust professional network. Remember that networking is not just about making connections; it's about cultivating relationships based on trust, mutual support, and shared goals. By approaching networking with the right mindset, you can unlock the power of your network and leverage it for long-term success.

2.2 Setting Networking Goals

Setting networking goals is an essential step in building an effective professional network. Without clear objectives in mind, networking can become aimless and unproductive. By setting specific goals, you can focus your efforts, prioritise your activities, and measure your progress. Here, we will dive deeper into the importance of setting networking goals and provide guidance on how to establish meaningful objectives for your networking endeavours.

Why Set Networking Goals?

1. Direction and Focus: Setting networking goals provides a sense of direction and purpose. It helps you understand what you want to achieve through networking, whether it is finding job opportunities, establishing partnerships, gaining industry insights, or building a supportive network. Having a clear focus enables you to streamline your efforts and make the most of your networking activities.

2. Motivation and Accountability: Goals provide motivation by giving you something to strive for and a sense of accomplishment when you reach them. They also hold you accountable for taking consistent action towards building your network. With measurable objectives in place, you can track your progress and make adjustments as needed.

3. Time Management: Networking can be time-consuming, especially if you don't have a specific plan in place. Setting goals allows you to prioritise your networking activities and allocate your time effectively. By identifying the most valuable connections to pursue and events to attend,

you can optimise your networking efforts without spreading yourself too thin.

4. Measuring Success: Goals provide a benchmark for measuring your networking success. They allow you to gauge your progress, identify areas for improvement, and celebrate your achievements. By tracking your accomplishments against your goals, you can gain valuable insights into the effectiveness of your networking strategies and make informed decisions for future endeavours.

How to Set Networking Goals

1. Determine Your Objectives: Start by identifying your overarching objectives for networking. Are you looking to advance in your current career, explore new job opportunities, gain industry knowledge, or establish connections for a future business venture? Having a clear focus will help you set specific goals aligned with your desired outcomes.

2. Make SMART Goals: Use the SMART framework (Specific, Measurable, Achievable, Relevant, Time-bound) to define your networking goals. Ensure they are well-defined, quantifiable, realistic, relevant to your aspirations, and time-bound. For example, instead of setting a vague

goal like "network more," strive for a specific, measurable objective such as "attend at least two industry conferences in the next six months to connect with potential collaborators and gain industry insights."

3. Break It Down: Break down your main networking goals into smaller, actionable steps. Determine the specific actions you need to take to achieve each goal. This could include attending networking events, joining professional associations, reaching out to industry experts for informational interviews, or participating in online networking groups.

4. Prioritise: Evaluate the importance and urgency of each goal to prioritise your networking activities. Determine which goals require immediate attention and which can be pursued over a longer period. By establishing priorities, you can allocate your time and resources accordingly and focus on the most critical objectives.

5. Create a Networking Plan: Develop a networking plan that outlines the specific actions you will take to achieve your goals. Include a timeline, milestones, and checkpoints to help you stay on track. Regularly review and update your plan as

needed to adapt to changing circumstances or new opportunities.

6. Measure and Evaluate: Regularly assess your progress against your networking goals. Monitor your achievements, evaluate the effectiveness of your strategies, and make any necessary adjustments. Celebrate milestones and use the insights gained from your evaluation to refine your networking approach and set new goals as you progress.

By setting clear and meaningful networking goals, you can channel your efforts towards building a robust and valuable professional network. Remember to be adaptable and open to new opportunities as you pursue your objectives and always maintain a genuine and authentic approach in your networking endeavours.

2.3 Identifying Target Connections

Identifying target connections in professional networking is a vital step in building a strong and effective network. These are the individuals who can provide value, support, and opportunities that align with your career goals and aspirations. Here is a comprehensive guide on how to identify and connect with your target audience in professional networking:

1. Define your goals: Start by clarifying your professional goals and objectives. Are you looking for mentorship, job opportunities, business partnerships, industry insights, or specific expertise? Understanding your goals will help you identify the type of connections you need to make.

2. Research your industry: Gain a deep understanding of your industry, including its key players, thought leaders, and influencers. Research trade associations, professional organisations, conferences, and events specific to your industry. This will give you insights into potential connections that hold relevance and influence within your industry.

3. Assess your skill gaps: Identify areas where you could benefit from knowledge, skills, or experience. Pinpoint the areas in which you need support, guidance, or expertise. This will help you seek connections who can provide valuable insights and assistance in your areas of need.

4. Leverage online platforms: Utilise professional networking platforms like LinkedIn, which offer

advanced search functionality to filter and identify connections based on industry, location, job title, company, and other relevant factors. LinkedIn also provides recommendations and insights on potential connections based on your existing network.

5. Engage in communities and forums: Participate in online communities, forums, and discussion groups related to your industry. Engaging in conversations, sharing knowledge, and offering support will help you discover like-minded professionals and potential connections who are active and influential in these communities.

6. Attend industry events: Regularly attend industry conferences, seminars, webinars, and networking events. These events provide opportunities to connect with professionals who are actively engaged in your industry and can offer insights, advice, and potential collaborations.

7. Seek referrals: Leverage your existing network for referrals and introductions. Reach out to trusted connections and express your goals and the types of connections you are seeking. They may be able to introduce you to individuals who can provide valuable insights or opportunities.

8. Personalise your approach: When reaching out to potential connections, take the time to personalise your messages and demonstrate a genuine interest in their work or achievements. Showing that you have done your research and that you value their expertise will increase the likelihood of establishing a meaningful and mutually beneficial connection.

Remember, building a professional network is a continuous process, and it requires time, persistence, and genuine effort. Continuously assess your networking goals and adjust your target connections accordingly. Nurture your relationships by offering support, sharing valuable resources, and keeping in touch. By building a network of targeted connections, you enhance your professional reputation, increase your opportunities for growth, and gain access to valuable insights and resources within your industry.

CHAPTER 3

Building and Maintaining a Professional Network

Building and maintaining a professional network is a vital aspect of career development and personal growth. It enables individuals to connect with others in their field, gain access to various resources and opportunities, and stay updated on industry trends. Below, we will discuss in detail the key steps and strategies involved in building and sustaining a professional network.

1. Set Networking Goals: Begin by defining your networking objectives. Determine what you hope to achieve through networking – whether it is seeking job opportunities, mentorship, industry insights, or collaborative partnerships. Having clear goals will help you focus your networking efforts and build meaningful connections.

2. Attend Networking Events: Actively participate in industry conferences, seminars, workshops, and other networking events. These events provide opportunities to meet professionals from diverse backgrounds who share common interests. Engage in conversations, inquire about others' experiences,

and actively listen. Be approachable, friendly, and open-minded, making it easier for others to connect with you.

3. Utilise Online Platforms: Leverage professional networking platforms such as LinkedIn, Twitter, and Facebook to expand your network beyond geographic boundaries. Regularly update your profiles, share valuable content, and engage in discussions. Connect with professionals in your field, join relevant groups, and actively contribute to conversations. Online platforms offer visibility, enhance your online presence, and help you connect with individuals you may not meet in person.

4. Seek Introductions and Referrals: Leverage your existing connections to make new ones. Reach out to trusted contacts and request introductions to individuals who can provide valuable insights or opportunities. Personal recommendations carry more weight and increase the likelihood of establishing fruitful connections. Additionally, reciprocate by offering to introduce your connections to those who may benefit from their expertise.

5. Provide Value: Networking is mutually beneficial, where you should aim to offer value to others. Share useful resources, offer assistance,

provide support, and contribute your expertise whenever possible. By providing value, you establish goodwill and develop stronger relationships within your network, increasing the chances of receiving support and opportunities in return.

6. Maintain Relationships: Building a network is not a one-time task; it requires consistent effort and maintenance. Regularly follow up with your connections through emails, phone calls, or in-person meetings. Stay updated on their professional endeavours, milestones, and challenges, and show genuine interest in their success. Remembering birthdays, work anniversaries, and milestones can also help solidify relationships and demonstrate your commitment to maintaining connections.

7. Join Professional Organizations and Associations: Become a member of industry-specific organisations and associations. These groups offer a focused platform for networking, professional development, and staying abreast of industry trends. Attend their events, participate in committees, and engage with other members. Active involvement in such organisations broadens your network and connects you with like-minded professionals.

8. Collaborate on Projects: Seek opportunities to collaborate with professionals in your field. Collaborative projects allow you to develop new skills, expand your knowledge, and demonstrate your expertise. Engaging in joint initiatives builds trust and strengthens your bond with others in your network, leading to long-lasting relationships and potential future collaborations.

9. Cultivate a Diverse Network: Aim to build a network that encompasses a diverse range of professionals. Connect with individuals from different industries, job roles, backgrounds, and experiences. A diverse network exposes you to new perspectives, ideas, and opportunities that may not exist within your immediate circle. Actively seek connections from various backgrounds and industries to broaden your horizons.

10. Maintain Professional Etiquette: Conduct yourself professionally in all networking interactions. Be prompt with your responses, respect others' time, and be mindful of your online presence. Upholding professional etiquette demonstrates your reliability, integrity, and commitment to maintaining fruitful connections within your network.

Building and maintaining a professional network is a continuous effort that requires proactive engagement and a genuine interest in others. Regularly reassess your networking goals, expand your network, and nurture meaningful connections. By investing time and energy in building a robust professional network, you enhance your career prospects, gain valuable industry insights, and establish a support system that will benefit you throughout your professional journey.

3.1 Creating a Powerful Personal Brand

In the realm of professional networking, creating a powerful personal brand is essential for making a lasting impression and standing out from the crowd. Your personal brand is essentially the way others perceive you and the value you bring to the table. It encompasses your reputation, expertise, and unique qualities that differentiate you from others in your field. Here, we delve into the strategies and techniques to create a powerful personal brand that will aid you in building and maintaining a strong professional network.

1. Define Your Professional Identity: Start by clearly defining your professional identity. What are your strengths, skills, and unique attributes that make you stand out? Identifying your core competencies and areas of expertise will help you shape your personal brand around what you bring to the table. Consider your past experiences, achievements, and the value you have added to your previous roles or projects. This will form the foundation of your personal brand.

2. Craft Your Personal Brand Statement: A personal brand statement succinctly communicates who you are, what you do, and the value you provide. It should be memorable, compelling, and capture the essence of your professional persona. For example, you might describe yourself as a "results-driven marketing strategist with a passion for data-driven decision making." Tailor your brand statement to reflect your expertise and the unique value you offer.

3. Develop a Consistent Online Presence: In this digital age, having a strong online presence is crucial for networking and connecting with professionals worldwide. Create a professional website or online portfolio to showcase your work, accomplishments, and expertise. Maintain active profiles on relevant social media platforms, such as

LinkedIn, Twitter, and industry-specific forums. Regularly update your profiles, share valuable content, and engage with your network to establish credibility and visibility.

4. Share Thought Leadership Content: Position yourself as an industry expert and thought leader by sharing valuable content related to your field. This can take the form of articles, blog posts, videos, podcasts, or social media updates. By sharing your insights and expertise, you establish yourself as a valuable resource and create opportunities for meaningful conversations with others in your industry. Consistently producing high-quality content demonstrates your commitment to staying at the forefront of your field.

5. Network Authentically: When networking, be authentic and genuine. Embrace your unique personality and let it shine through in your interactions. Avoid trying to be someone you're not or mimicking others. Authenticity helps build trust and fosters genuine connections. People are more likely to remember and refer someone who is true to themselves and transparent in their professional dealings.

6. Cultivate Your Online Reputation: Manage your online reputation by actively monitoring and

responding to feedback, reviews, and comments. Engage with others in a respectful and professional manner. Respond to inquiries promptly, address concerns, and express gratitude for positive feedback. Maintaining a positive online reputation enhances your credibility and fosters trust within your network.

7. Seek Endorsements and Recommendations: Endorsements and recommendations from peers, colleagues, clients, or mentors can greatly enhance your personal brand. Request testimonials from individuals who have seen firsthand the value you bring to your work. Display these recommendations on your website, LinkedIn profile, or other professional platforms. Positive endorsements can strengthen your personal brand and build trust with potential connections.

8. Be Visible and Proactive: Actively participate in industry events, conferences, webinars, and online discussions. Offer to speak at conferences or contribute guest articles to reputable publications. By putting yourself out there, you increase your visibility and establish yourself as an active contributor within your field.

9. Embrace Continuous Learning: To maintain a powerful personal brand, embrace continuous

learning and professional development. Stay updated on industry trends, advancements, and best practices. Attend workshops, webinars, and training programs to expand your skill set and demonstrate your commitment to staying relevant. A lifelong learner is seen as someone who is invested in their field and continuously strives for improvement.

10. Live Your Brand: Finally, live your personal brand consistently in everything you do. Your actions, ethics, and achievements should align with the image and values you project through your personal brand. Strive for excellence in your work, treat others with respect, and consistently deliver high-quality results. By walking the talk, you reinforce your personal brand and build a network of professionals who trust and admire your authenticity.

Creating a powerful personal brand is a process that requires self-reflection, refinement, and consistency. By intentionally shaping your brand and aligning it with your professional goals and values, you position yourself as a valuable asset to your network. A strong personal brand not only attracts connections but also helps you navigate the professional landscape with confidence and credibility, leading to increased opportunities for growth and success.

3.2 Leveraging Social Media for Networking

In today's digital age, social media has emerged as a powerful tool for networking and connecting with professionals across various industries. Leveraging social media platforms effectively can significantly enhance your professional network and open doors to new opportunities. In this section, we explore the strategies and best practices for harnessing the power of social media for networking.

1. Choose the Right Platforms: Start by carefully selecting the social media platforms that align with your professional goals and target audience. LinkedIn, the leading professional networking platform, is essential for building online connections, sharing industry insights, and showcasing your expertise. Additionally, consider platforms such as Twitter, Facebook, Instagram, and industry-specific forums or groups where professionals in your field gather.

2. Optimise Your Profiles: Ensure your social media profiles are complete, up to date, and accurately reflect your personal brand. Use a professional headshot as your profile picture and craft a

compelling headline that showcases your expertise and value proposition. Write a concise and engaging summary that highlights your key qualifications, skills, and achievements. Make use of relevant keywords related to your field to improve your visibility in search results.

3. Expand Your Network: Actively seek out professionals in your industry and connect with them on social media. Send personalised connection requests that specify why you are interested in connecting with them. Look for thought leaders, influencers, and experts in your field, as well as potential mentors or individuals who work in companies or organisations that align with your professional goals.

4. Engage in Conversations: Don't simply rely on connecting with others passively. Engage in meaningful conversations by commenting, liking, and sharing content that resonates with you. Share your insights and expertise through thoughtful comments and replies. Actively participating in industry-related discussions positions you as an active and engaged professional within your field.

5. Share Valuable Content: Demonstrate your knowledge and expertise by regularly sharing valuable content on your social media profiles. This

can include articles, blog posts, industry news, videos, podcasts, or even your own original content. Share content that provides insights, educates, or sparks meaningful discussions. Consistency is key; aim to maintain a regular posting schedule to stay on top of mind with your connections.

6. Join and Engage in Groups: Participating in relevant professional groups or communities within your industry provides excellent networking opportunities. Join groups on platforms like LinkedIn or Facebook where professionals in your niche gather to discuss industry trends, challenges, and opportunities. Contribute to discussions, answer questions, and share your expertise. This not only helps you expand your network but also positions you as a knowledgeable and valuable resource.

7. Utilise Advanced Search Features: Take advantage of the advanced search features available on social media platforms, especially on LinkedIn. These features allow you to narrow down your search and find professionals based on specific criteria such as job title, industry, location, or company. This can be particularly useful when seeking connections in a specific industry or targeting individuals who work in certain organisations.

8. Attend Virtual Events and Webinars: Many professional associations and organisations now host virtual events and webinars that offer networking opportunities. Participate actively in these events, ask questions, and contribute to discussions. Use the chat or messaging features to connect with other attendees and speakers. Virtual events provide a unique opportunity to network with professionals from around the world without the limitations of geographical boundaries.

9. Share Your Successes and Achievements: Celebrate your professional milestones and accomplishments on social media. Share updates about projects you've completed, awards or recognition you've received, or any significant milestones that highlight your expertise and competence. This helps build credibility and attracts the attention of potential collaborators or opportunities.

10. Maintain Professionalism and Etiquette: While social media offers a more informal and relaxed platform for networking, it's essential to maintain professionalism and adhere to networking etiquette. Be respectful in your interactions, avoid controversial or divisive topics, and refrain from engaging in negative or contentious discussions. Remember that your online presence can have a

lasting impact on your professional reputation, so always conduct yourself with professionalism and integrity.

Leveraging social media for networking allows you to connect with professionals globally, gain visibility in your industry, and stay up to date with the latest trends and developments. By following these strategies and best practices, you can harness the power of social media to build a strong professional network that supports your career growth and opens doors to new opportunities.

3.3 Attending Networking Events and Conferences

Attending networking events and conferences is a valuable opportunity to meet professionals from various industries, build connections, and expand your professional network. These events provide a platform for like-minded individuals to gather, share insights, exchange ideas, and explore potential collaboration or career opportunities. In this section, we explore the benefits of attending networking events and conferences and provide strategies for maximising your experience.

Benefits of Attending Networking Events and Conferences:

1. Expand Your Network: Networking events and conferences bring together professionals from diverse backgrounds and industries. Attending these events allows you to connect with individuals you may not typically encounter in your daily professional life. By expanding your network, you increase the chances of discovering new perspectives, potential clients, mentors, job opportunities, or even business partners.

2. Stay Informed: Networking events and conferences often feature keynote speakers, panel discussions, or workshops where industry experts share their experiences and insights. Attending these sessions helps you stay updated on the latest industry trends, advancements, challenges, and best practices. This knowledge not only enhances your professional development but also positions you as a knowledgeable and informed professional within your field.

3. Exchange Ideas and Gain Fresh Perspectives: Networking events provide a platform for interactive discussions and knowledge sharing. Engaging in conversations with professionals from diverse backgrounds allows you to exchange ideas,

gain different perspectives, and challenge your own thinking. This can spark creativity, innovation, and open doors to new opportunities or collaborations you may not have considered before.

4. Build Relationships Face-to-Face: While online networking is valuable, face-to-face interactions create a more personal and lasting impression. Attending networking events gives you the opportunity to meet people in person, have meaningful conversations, and build deeper connections. Establishing a personal rapport and connection can lead to long-term professional relationships and collaborations.

Strategies for Maximising Networking Events:

1. Set Clear Objectives: Before attending a networking event or conference, set clear objectives for what you hope to achieve. Whether it's connecting with professionals in a specific industry, finding potential mentors, or seeking career opportunities, having a clear focus will help you make the most of your time and efforts.

2. Research and Plan: Prior to the event, research the speakers, panellists, and attendees to identify key individuals you want to connect with. Prepare thoughtful questions or conversation starters to

initiate meaningful discussions. Create a schedule or plan your agenda for the event, ensuring that you allocate time for networking, attending sessions, and engaging with exhibitors or sponsors.

3. Be Approachable and Engaging: Approach networking events with an open mindset and a positive attitude. Smile, maintain eye contact, and be approachable. Actively listen and show genuine interest in others when engaging in conversations. Be prepared with a concise and engaging introduction that highlights your expertise and what you are looking to gain from the event.

4. Attend Interactive Sessions and Workshops: Make the most of the educational opportunities provided by networking events. Attend sessions, workshops, or panel discussions relevant to your professional interests. Ask insightful questions, contribute to discussions, and share your own experiences or insights. This positions you as an active participant and increases your visibility among the attendees.

5. Utilise Networking Tools and Apps: Some networking events provide tools or apps that help attendees connect with each other. Take advantage of these tools to find and connect with professionals who share your interests or belong to your target

industry. Utilise the event's networking platform or app to schedule meetings, exchange contact information, or share resources.

6. Follow Up and Nurture Relationships: After attending a networking event, promptly follow up with the individuals you connected with. Send personalised follow-up emails expressing your pleasure in meeting them and referencing specific topics or discussions you had. Offer to connect on social media platforms or schedule further conversations to explore potential collaborations or opportunities. Nurturing these relationships is essential for long-term networking success.

Attending networking events and conferences provides a unique opportunity to build connections, gain industry insights, and explore potential opportunities. By setting clear objectives, planning ahead, engaging in meaningful conversations, and nurturing relationships, you can maximise the value of these events and enhance your professional network for future success.

3.4 Joining Professional Associations and Organizations

Joining professional associations and organisations is an effective way to build and expand your professional network. These groups bring together individuals with similar interests, expertise, and aspirations, providing opportunities for collaboration, knowledge sharing, and career advancement. In this section, we explore the benefits of joining professional associations and organisations and provide strategies for getting the most out of your membership.

Benefits of Joining Professional Associations and Organisations:

1. Access to a Diverse Network: Professional associations and organisations bring together individuals from various industries, backgrounds, and levels of experience. By joining these groups, you gain access to a diverse network of professionals who can offer different perspectives, insights, and opportunities. This diversity enhances your own knowledge, widens your professional network, and increases your chances of finding mentors, advisors, or potential collaborators.

2. Professional Development Opportunities: Professional associations and organisations often provide members with access to educational resources, workshops, conferences, and training sessions. Engaging in these activities helps you stay updated on industry trends, advancements, and best practices. It also allows you to enhance your skills, expand your knowledge base, and position yourself as a knowledgeable professional within your field.

3. Career Advancement: Membership in professional associations and organisations can enhance your career prospects by providing access to job boards, career development resources, and networking events specifically tailored to your industry. These groups may also offer mentoring programs, leadership opportunities, or awards recognition that can boost your professional profile and open doors to new career opportunities.

4. Advocacy and Influencing Policy: Many professional associations and organisations work towards advancing the interests of their members and the industry as a whole. By joining these groups, you can contribute to shaping industry policies, standards, and regulations. Active involvement in advocacy efforts not only demonstrates your commitment and expertise within your field but also provides opportunities to

influence decision-making and contribute to the growth and development of your profession.

Strategies for Getting the Most out of Professional Associations and Organisations:

1. Research and Select the Right Groups: Conduct research to identify professional associations and organisations that align with your industry, interests, and career goals. Consider factors such as the reputation, size, and focus of the group. Look for associations that offer relevant resources, networking opportunities, and professional development programs. Evaluate the benefits of membership and compare membership fees to ensure they match your expectations and budget.

2. Attend Events and Engage Actively: Once you have joined a professional association or organisation, actively participate in their events, conferences, workshops, and networking sessions. Attend industry-specific conferences, seminars, or panel discussions to enhance your knowledge and meet professionals in your field. Actively engage in discussions, ask questions, and offer your own perspectives to make the most of these opportunities.

3. Volunteer and Take on Leadership Roles: Embrace opportunities to volunteer for committees, task forces, or leadership positions within your professional association or organisation. By actively contributing and taking on responsibilities, you increase your visibility, expand your network, and gain valuable leadership and managerial skills. Additionally, serving in a leadership role allows you to shape the direction of the organisation and contribute to its growth and success.

4. Utilise Online Platforms and Resources: Many professional associations and organisations provide online platforms or member-exclusive resources such as forums, webinars, or discussion boards. Take advantage of these platforms to connect with other members, seek advice, share insights, and collaborate on projects or initiatives. Actively contribute to these platforms by sharing your expertise, participating in discussions, and offering support to fellow members.

5. Network and Build Relationships: In addition to participating in association events, take the initiative to network with fellow members. Attend networking sessions, connect with members on social media, and arrange one-on-one meetings to build relationships. It is important to cultivate meaningful connections by actively listening,

showing an interest in others' work, and offering your support whenever possible.

6. Stay Involved and Engaged: As a member of a professional association or organisation, make a commitment to stay involved and engaged. Continuously attend events, contribute to initiatives, and take advantage of learning opportunities. Regularly review and utilise the benefits and resources provided to members. By remaining active and engaged, you maximise the value of your membership and strengthen your professional network.

Joining professional associations and organisations can significantly enhance your professional network, provide opportunities for professional development, and advance your career. By selecting the right groups, actively engaging in their activities, and building genuine relationships, you can make the most of your membership and leverage these platforms to achieve your professional goals.

3.5 Nurturing Relationships Through Effective Communication

Effective communication is crucial for nurturing relationships within your professional network. Building connections is not just about making initial contacts; it requires consistent and meaningful interaction to maintain and strengthen those relationships over time. In this section, we explore strategies for nurturing relationships through effective communication.

1. Regular and Timely Communication: In order to maintain relationships, it is important to stay in touch with your contacts on a regular basis. This can be achieved through various channels such as emails, phone calls, social media messages, or in-person meetings. Regular check-ins and updates show your interest and dedication to the relationship. Additionally, responding to communication in a timely manner demonstrates respect for the other person's time and priorities.

2. Personalise Your Communication: Tailor your communication to each individual based on their preferences and interests. Personalization shows that you value the relationship and are willing to make an effort to understand and connect with the other person on a deeper level. This can include

referencing past conversations, acknowledging their achievements or milestones, or sharing relevant articles or resources that may be of interest to them.

3. Active Listening: Effective communication is not just about speaking, but also about actively listening to the other person. When engaging in conversations, be attentive and show genuine interest in what the other person has to say. Avoid interrupting and instead, ask open-ended questions to encourage them to share more about their experiences, challenges, and goals. This demonstrates your interest in their perspectives and helps to build trust and rapport.

4. Show Appreciation and Gratitude: Take the time to acknowledge and appreciate the contributions and support of your network. Expressing gratitude for their help, advice, or referrals can go a long way in nurturing relationships. This can be done through a simple thank-you email, a handwritten note, or a small gesture of appreciation such as sending a token of gratitude or recommending their services to others.

5. Provide Value: In order to build strong relationships, it is important to be a valuable resource to your network. This can be achieved by sharing relevant information, insights, or resources

that can benefit them professionally. For example, you can send articles, attend conferences or seminars together, provide introductions to other contacts, or offer your expertise and assistance when needed.

6. Be Authentic and Transparent: Building trust is essential in nurturing professional relationships. Being authentic and transparent in your communication helps to foster genuine connections. Avoid exaggerating or misleading information and instead, be honest and genuine in your interactions. This allows others to trust and rely on you, which is vital for long-term relationship building.

7. Follow Up and Follow Through: Whenever you make a commitment or promise to your network, ensure that you follow up and follow through on your commitments. This demonstrates reliability and professionalism, reinforcing the trust and credibility you have established. If you have made a promise to connect them with someone or provide assistance, make sure to take action in a timely manner.

8. Use Technology Wisely: With the advancements in technology, there are numerous tools and platforms available for communication. Utilise technology wisely to enhance your communication

and relationship-building efforts. However, it is important to maintain a balance and not rely solely on technology. Whenever possible, opt for face-to-face or voice-to-voice interactions, as they allow for a more personal and meaningful connection.

Remember, effective communication is a two-way street. It involves actively listening, showing interest, providing value, and establishing trust. By consistently nurturing relationships through effective communication, you can strengthen your professional network, foster mutual support, and open doors to new opportunities for success.

3.6 Building a Network of Mentors and Advisors

Building a network of mentors and advisors is a crucial aspect of professional networking as it can provide guidance, support, and valuable insights throughout your career journey. Mentors and advisors are experienced professionals who can offer advice, share their industry knowledge, and help you navigate various challenges and decisions. In this section, we delve into the importance of building a network of mentors and advisors and explore strategies for finding and nurturing these relationships.

1. The Importance of Mentors and Advisors: Mentors and advisors play a critical role in professional development and growth. They offer guidance, serve as a sounding board for ideas and decisions, provide constructive feedback, and share their own experiences and lessons learned. Having access to the wisdom and expertise of seasoned professionals can help you gain insights, avoid common pitfalls, and make well-informed decisions in your career.

2. Identifying Potential Mentors and Advisors: Begin by identifying individuals who possess the skills, knowledge, and experience that align with your goals and aspirations. Look for professionals who are respected in your industry or field of interest and who have a track record of success. Consider reaching out to individuals who have achieved what you aspire to achieve or who have expertise in areas you want to develop. Mentors and advisors can come from diverse backgrounds and can include senior leaders in your organisation, industry experts, professors or instructors, or even experienced colleagues.

3. Approaching Potential Mentors and Advisors: When approaching potential mentors and advisors, it is important to be respectful and considerate of their time and commitments. Begin by researching their background and accomplishments to demonstrate your genuine interest and admiration for their expertise. Craft a thoughtful and personalised introduction, expressing your admiration and explaining why you believe their guidance would be valuable to your professional journey. Be clear about your expectations and the areas in which you would like their support. Requesting a brief meeting or informational interview can be a good starting point.

4. Developing a Trusting Relationship: Once you have established a mentor or advisor relationship, focus on building trust and rapport. Approach the relationship with humility, respect, and a willingness to listen and learn. Be open and receptive to their feedback and guidance, demonstrating your commitment to growth and improvement. Regularly update them on your progress, seek their input on important decisions, and show appreciation for their time and support.

5. Establishing Clear Expectations: Set clear expectations for your mentor or advisor relationship. Clearly define the areas in which you

seek support and guidance, whether it is career growth, skill development, or navigating specific challenges. Understand that the relationship should be mutually beneficial, and strive to contribute to your mentor or advisor's growth as well. Discuss the frequency and format of meetings or interactions, and be respectful of boundaries and time commitments.

6. Nurturing the Relationship: Like any relationship, a mentor or advisor relationship requires ongoing nurturing and maintenance. Regularly check in with your mentor or advisor to provide updates on your progress, seek their advice on new challenges, and express your gratitude for their continued support. Share your successes and challenges, and be open to receiving feedback and constructive criticism. Actively incorporate their advice and guidance into your professional development plans.

7. Expanding and Diversifying Your Network: While a mentor or advisor relationship can provide immense value, it is essential to continue expanding and diversifying your network of mentors and advisors. Seek out individuals with different perspectives, experiences, and expertise to gain a well-rounded understanding of your industry and profession. Consider joining mentorship programs or organisations that facilitate connections with

potential mentors and advisors. Actively pursue opportunities to connect with professionals through networking events, conferences, or online platforms.

Remember, building a network of mentors and advisors is not just about finding support, but also about fostering relationships based on mutual trust, respect, and growth. By investing in these relationships, you can gain valuable insights, expand your professional network, and enhance your chances for long-term success in your career.

CHAPTER 4

Networking Strategies for Different Scenarios

Networking strategies can vary depending on the specific scenario you find yourself in. Whether you are networking within the workplace, aiming for career advancement, starting a business, seeking a job, or navigating the digital realm, understanding the strategies best suited for each scenario is essential. Here, we explore networking strategies for these different situations:

4.1 Networking within the Workplace

Networking within the workplace is a crucial aspect of professional growth and success. By developing connections within your organisation, you can gain valuable insights, create collaborations, and open doors for career advancement. Here, we will explore effective networking strategies specific to the workplace environment.

To network successfully within the workplace, it is important to:

1. Establish a positive presence: Make a conscious effort to interact with colleagues from different departments and levels within the organisation. Attend social events, team-building activities, and office gatherings to create opportunities for connection.

2. Seek out mentors and advocates: Identifying senior professionals who can guide and support your career growth can significantly enhance your networking efforts. Seek mentors who can offer advice, share their experiences, and advocate for your professional development within the company.

3. Volunteering for cross-functional projects: Engaging in projects that span across different departments allows you to collaborate with colleagues from diverse backgrounds. By demonstrating your skills, work ethic, and ability to work well with others, you can expand your network and create positive impressions.

4. Participate in internal initiatives: Take advantage of internal initiatives such as learning and development programs, employee resource groups, and committees. Engaging in these activities not only expands your network but also demonstrates your commitment to the organisation.

5. Take the initiative to connect: Do not hesitate to introduce yourself to new colleagues, invite them for coffee or lunch, and have conversations that go beyond work-related topics. Building genuine relationships with your peers creates a supportive network that can help you navigate challenges and open doors to new opportunities.

6. Sharing knowledge and expertise: Be generous with sharing your knowledge and expertise within the organisation. Offer assistance, provide valuable insights, and be a resource for your colleagues. This not only strengthens your personal brand but also establishes you as a valuable member of the team.

7. Stay visible and engaged: Actively participate in meetings, contribute ideas, and offer your perspective on important matters. By demonstrating your commitment and enthusiasm, you increase your visibility within the organisation, making it easier for others to remember and recommend you for future opportunities.

8. Attend professional development programs: Take advantage of training and development programs offered by your organisation. These programs allow you to connect with professionals from different departments and gain valuable skills, all while expanding your network.

9. Show gratitude and appreciation: Acknowledge and appreciate the efforts and achievements of your colleagues. Taking the time to express your gratitude creates a positive impression and strengthens your professional relationships.

10. Maintain a positive online presence: Utilise internal communication platforms, such as intranets or online collaboration tools, to contribute to discussions and showcase your expertise. Additionally, maintain an updated and professional profile on LinkedIn, highlighting your skills, accomplishments, and experiences.

Remember, networking within the workplace is not just about expanding your contacts but also about building genuine relationships based on trust and mutual support. By investing time and effort into fostering these connections, you can create a network that can propel your professional growth and contribute to your overall success within the organisation.

4.2　　Networking　　for　　Career Advancement

Networking plays a vital role in career advancement by providing opportunities for growth, skill development, and visibility within your industry. Building a strong professional network can help you access job openings, gain industry insights, and receive mentorship and guidance. In this section, we will explore effective networking strategies for career advancement.

1. Define your career goals: Before you begin networking for career advancement, it is essential to have a clear understanding of your career goals. Identify the specific skills, experiences, or positions you aim to achieve. This clarity will guide your networking efforts and help you connect with individuals who can support your career aspirations.

2. Attend industry events and conferences: Industry-specific events, conferences, and seminars are excellent platforms for networking. Attend these events regularly to meet professionals from various organisations within your industry. Engage in conversations, exchange business cards, and make a positive impression by showcasing your expertise and passion for your field.

3. Join professional associations and organisations: Professional associations often host events, workshops, and forums that provide opportunities for networking. Become a member of relevant associations in your field and actively participate in their activities. This involvement allows you to connect with industry leaders and professionals who can provide valuable insights and guidance.

4. Seek mentorship and guidance: Developing professional relationships with mentors is invaluable for career advancement. Look for individuals in your field who have achieved success and seek their guidance. Reach out to them, express your admiration for their accomplishments, and request their mentorship. Their advice and support can help you navigate obstacles and seize opportunities.

5. Utilise digital networking platforms: In the digital age, online platforms have become essential for networking. Create a strong and professional presence on platforms like LinkedIn by regularly sharing industry insights, participating in group discussions, and reaching out to professionals with personalised messages. These platforms provide a vast pool of professionals that you can connect with to expand your network.

6. Engage in informational interviews: Informational interviews are opportunities to connect with professionals in senior positions to learn from their experiences and gain knowledge about your industry. Request short meetings with individuals whose careers you admire, ask thoughtful questions, and show genuine interest in their insights. These conversations can provide valuable guidance and may even lead to job openings or recommendations.

7. Volunteer or participate in community initiatives: Participating in community initiatives within your industry can broaden your network and showcase your passion and commitment. Volunteer for committees, boards, or projects where you can collaborate with professionals from diverse backgrounds. This involvement not only expands your network but also demonstrates your dedication to the growth and development of your industry.

8. Share your expertise: Position yourself as a valuable resource by sharing your industry knowledge and expertise. Write articles, publish blog posts, or speak at industry events to establish yourself as a subject matter expert. This visibility not only enhances your personal brand but also attracts opportunities for career advancement.

9. Maintain and nurture your network: Networking is not a one-time event; it requires consistent effort and nurturing. Reach out to your network regularly, offer assistance, congratulate them on their achievements, and stay connected through social media or occasional meetings. Cultivating genuine and long-lasting relationships is essential for career advancement.

10. Pay it forward: As you advance in your career, remember to support and mentor other professionals. Offer guidance, share opportunities, and be a connector in your network. By paying it forward, you contribute to the growth and success of your industry, while also nurturing relationships that may benefit you in the future.

Networking for career advancement is a continuous process that requires both proactivity and authenticity. By leveraging various networking strategies and consistently investing in building and maintaining relationships, you can create a strong network that supports your professional growth and propels you towards success in your career.

4.3 Networking as an Entrepreneur or Small Business Owner

As an entrepreneur or small business owner, networking plays a vital role in building and growing your business. Connecting with other professionals, potential clients, and industry experts can open doors to new opportunities, partnerships, and collaborations. In section 4.3 of this book, we will delve into various networking strategies specifically tailored to entrepreneurs and small business owners.

Networking within the entrepreneurial community is essential for sharing knowledge, experiences, and resources. By attending industry-specific events, such as conferences, workshops, and meetups, entrepreneurs can meet like-minded individuals, exchange ideas, and gain valuable insights. These events provide opportunities to learn from successful entrepreneurs, investors, and innovators, inspiring and motivating individuals to further develop their business ventures.

Networking as an entrepreneur also involves joining relevant professional associations and organisations. These groups can provide a platform to showcase your expertise, connect with potential partners or clients, and gain industry recognition. Participating in networking events organised by these associations allows entrepreneurs to engage with key influencers and stay up-to-date with industry trends and developments.

A powerful personal brand is crucial for entrepreneurs and small business owners. Section 3.1 of this book highlights the importance of creating a unique personal brand. This brand serves as your identity and differentiates you from competitors. When networking, having a strong personal brand helps attract attention and instil confidence in potential connections.

Social media platforms can be immensely valuable for entrepreneurs when it comes to networking. Section 3.2 discusses leveraging social media platforms for networking purposes. Platforms like LinkedIn provide a means to connect with industry professionals, potential clients, and even investors. Actively engaging in relevant conversations, sharing insightful content, and maintaining an online presence can foster meaningful connections and drive business growth.

In addition to offline events and online platforms, entrepreneurs should also focus on building a network of mentors and advisors. Section 3.6 explains the importance of mentors and advisors in a professional network. Seasoned entrepreneurs who have navigated the challenges of starting and growing a business can provide invaluable guidance and support. Leveraging the knowledge and experiences of mentors can help entrepreneurs avoid common pitfalls and make informed decisions.

In the digital age, an increasing number of entrepreneurs are harnessing the power of online platforms and virtual connections. Section 4.5 explores networking in the digital age. Webinars, online forums, and virtual conferences enable entrepreneurs to connect with a vast network of individuals from around the world. These platforms provide flexibility and convenience, allowing entrepreneurs to build connections without geographical constraints.

Networking as an entrepreneur or small business owner comes with its own set of challenges. Overcoming fear and shyness, building authentic connections, and managing time efficiently are all obstacles that entrepreneurs may face when networking. Chapter 5 of this book explores strategies for overcoming such challenges and maximising networking opportunities.

Networking is a critical component of success for entrepreneurs and small business owners. By actively participating in networking events, leveraging social media, and building a network of mentors, entrepreneurs can unlock invaluable opportunities, gain industry insights, and establish their businesses in a competitive landscape. Embracing networking as an essential business strategy will undoubtedly contribute to long-term success.

4.4 Networking for Job Seekers and Career Changers

Finding a job can be a challenging and overwhelming process, especially in competitive industries. However, one of the most effective strategies for job seekers and career changers is networking. By building connections and leveraging personal relationships, individuals can access hidden job markets, gain valuable insights, and increase their chances of finding the right job or transitioning into a new career. This section will explore networking strategies specifically tailored for job seekers and career changers.

Understanding the Importance of Networking for Job Seekers and Career Changers

Networking plays a critical role in the job search process as it allows individuals to tap into the hidden job market. Many job opportunities are never advertised, and are instead filled through referrals or recommendations from personal connections. By actively networking, job seekers and career changers can gain access to these unadvertised opportunities, increasing their chances of finding suitable positions.

Additionally, networking provides job seekers and career changers with valuable insights and information about industries, companies, and roles. Speaking with professionals currently working in their desired field can help individuals determine if a particular career path is the right fit for them. Informational interviews, attending industry events, and joining professional associations are great networking strategies to gather insights and build knowledge.

Networking Strategies for Job Seekers and Career Changers
Networking strategies for job seekers and career changers may differ slightly from general networking approaches. Here are some effective strategies to consider:

a. Informational Interviews: Reach out to professionals in your desired field and request informational interviews. These meetings provide an opportunity to learn more about the industry or role, gain insights into the job market, and potentially build relationships that could lead to job opportunities.

b. Attend Job Fairs and Industry Events: Job fairs and industry events bring together professionals and employers from various industries. Attending these events allows job seekers and career changers to network directly with companies and recruiters, increasing their visibility and access to potential job opportunities.

c. Utilise Online Platforms: Online platforms such as LinkedIn can be powerful tools for job seekers and career changers. Create a strong and professional profile, join relevant groups, and actively engage with professionals in your desired field. Engaging through comments, sharing industry insights, and participating in discussions can help you build connections and increase visibility to potential employers.

d. Leverage Alumni Networks: Connect with alumni from your alma mater who are working in your desired field or industry. Alumni networks often have dedicated platforms or events where individuals can connect and network. These connections can provide valuable advice, referrals, or even job opportunities.

e. Professional Associations and Industry Organizations: Joining professional associations and industry organisations provides an excellent networking opportunity. Attend their networking events, workshops, and conferences to meet professionals in your desired field and stay updated on industry trends.

Nurturing and Leveraging Relationships
Building a network is not only about making initial connections but also about nurturing and leveraging those relationships effectively. Here are some tips to consider:

a. Follow up: Always follow up with individuals you have connected with, whether it's through a thank you note, email, or LinkedIn message. This demonstrates your sincerity and helps solidify the relationship.

b. Provide Value: Networking is a two-way street. Look for opportunities to offer assistance or provide value to the individuals in your network. Share industry insights, make relevant introductions, or offer to help with projects. By being generous with your time and expertise, you can build stronger and more meaningful connections.

c. Stay Connected: Keep in touch with your network on a regular basis, even if you are not actively job searching or changing careers. Connect through social media, attend industry events together, or schedule catch-up meetings. Maintaining active relationships ensures that when you are ready to make a move, your network is there to support and guide you.

d. Leverage Referrals: When you come across job opportunities or career prospects that may be suitable for individuals in your network, refer or recommend them. These referrals can strengthen your relationships and encourage others to think of you when they come across potential opportunities.

Overcoming Challenges and Staying Resilient
The job search or career change process can be filled with setbacks and challenges. It's essential to stay resilient and maintain a positive mindset. Here are some tips for overcoming common networking challenges:

a. Embrace Rejections: Rejections are a natural part of the job search process. Don't let them discourage you. Instead, view them as learning opportunities and keep refining your approach.

b. Be Persistent: Networking is not a one-time effort; it requires consistent effort and persistence. Keep reaching out to professionals, attending industry events, and staying active on online platforms. Slowly but surely, your efforts will pay off.

c. Seek Support: Building a support system of friends, family, and fellow job seekers can provide the emotional support needed during the job search or career change process. Lean on your support system when faced with challenges, and seek guidance and advice.

d. Continuously Improve: Be open to learning from your networking experiences. Reflect on what works and what doesn't, and continually adapt your networking strategies accordingly. Continuous improvement is key to building a successful network.

Networking is an essential tool for job seekers and career changers. By actively building connections, individuals can access hidden job markets, gain valuable insights, and increase their chances of finding suitable positions. By implementing effective networking strategies, nurturing relationships, and staying resilient, job seekers and career changers can unlock new opportunities and pave their paths to success. Networking is not only about finding a job but also about building a solid foundation for long-term career growth and development.

4.5 Networking in the Digital Age: Online Platforms and Virtual Connections

In the digital age, technology has transformed the way we connect and communicate with others. Online platforms and virtual connections have become powerful tools for professional networking. In this section, we will explore the strategies and benefits of networking in the digital age.

One of the most effective online platforms for professional networking is LinkedIn. With over 700 million users worldwide, LinkedIn provides a platform for professionals to showcase their skills, experience, and expertise. By creating a compelling profile, professionals can attract the attention of potential partners, clients, and even employers. LinkedIn also offers various groups and communities where individuals can engage in discussions, share insights, and expand their network.

Beyond LinkedIn, other social media platforms such as Twitter and Instagram can also be utilised for networking purposes. These platforms provide opportunities to connect with industry influencers, stay updated on industry news and trends, and engage in conversations with professionals around the world. By actively sharing valuable content, participating in relevant hashtag conversations, and engaging with others' posts, professionals can enhance their visibility and establish their expertise within their respective fields.

Virtual connections, facilitated by video conferencing platforms like Zoom and Microsoft Teams, have become increasingly common in today's digital landscape. Virtual conferences, webinars, and online networking events offer convenience and flexibility for professionals to connect with others from the comfort of their homes or offices. These virtual interactions allow for global networking, enabling professionals to connect with individuals from different geographical locations and expand their network beyond what is possible in traditional face-to-face settings.

One of the advantages of networking in the digital age is the ability to establish connections with industry experts and thought leaders. Many professionals are now accessible through platforms like LinkedIn or Twitter, where they actively share insights and engage with their audience. Engaging with these influencers by commenting on their posts, sharing their content, and reaching out for advice or collaboration opportunities can open doors to mentorship, partnership, and even speaking engagements.

With the convenience of online platforms, networking in the digital age also allows professionals to efficiently connect with a diverse group of individuals. Geographical boundaries no longer limit networking opportunities, enabling professionals from different countries, cultures, and backgrounds to collaborate and learn from each other. This diversity can lead to the exchange of ideas, perspectives, and best practices, ultimately enhancing personal and professional growth.

However, networking in the digital age also comes with its challenges. Building authentic connections in a virtual setting can be more challenging compared to face-to-face interactions. Professionals need to make an effort to connect on a personal level by sharing genuine insights, offering support, and showing interest in others' work. Additionally, managing online presence and ensuring a professional online reputation requires thoughtfulness and strategic content sharing.

Networking in the digital age through online platforms and virtual connections has revolutionised professional networking. Utilising platforms like LinkedIn, Twitter, and virtual conferencing tools, professionals can expand their network, connect with industry leaders, and access global opportunities. It is essential to leverage these digital tools while also maintaining authenticity, engagement, and professionalism to maximise the benefits of networking in the digital age.

CHAPTER 5

Overcoming Networking Challenges and Obstacles

Networking can be an invaluable tool for professional success, but it is not without its challenges and obstacles. These challenges can range from overcoming fear and shyness to managing time and dealing with rejection. In this section, we will explore strategies for overcoming these obstacles and enhancing your networking skills.

5.1 Overcoming Fear and Shyness in Networking

Fear and shyness can be significant obstacles when it comes to networking. The thought of initiating conversations with strangers or approaching influential individuals can be daunting. However, it is essential to overcome these fears to unlock the full potential of networking for professional growth. Here are some strategies to help overcome fear and shyness in networking:

1. Change Your Mindset: Instead of seeing networking as a daunting task, reframe it as an opportunity for personal and professional growth. Recognize that networking is about building connections and learning from others. Focus on the value that networking can bring to your career.

2. Prepare in Advance: Preparation can help boost your confidence and alleviate anxiety. Research the people you want to connect with, such as their professional background, current projects, or areas of expertise. This knowledge will provide you with conversation starters and make you feel more prepared and comfortable approaching them.

3. Start Small: If the idea of networking with a large group of people makes you nervous, start by networking with individuals you feel more comfortable with. Begin with your friends, colleagues, or acquaintances and gradually expand your network to include new individuals and groups.

4. Practise Active Listening: One way to overcome shyness is to focus on actively listening to others instead of worrying about what you will say next. By genuinely listening to the person you are conversing with, you can make a genuine connection and demonstrate that you value their

perspective. This will create a more engaging and comfortable conversation for both parties involved.

5. Attend Networking Workshops or Training Sessions: Participating in networking workshops or training sessions can provide you with valuable techniques and tools to overcome your fear and shyness. These sessions often involve practising networking skills in a supportive environment, offering you an opportunity to develop your networking abilities and build confidence.

6. Utilise Ice Breakers: Ice breakers are simple conversation starters that can help initiate a discussion and break down barriers. Develop a repertoire of ice breaker questions or statements that you feel comfortable using. These can include topics related to current events, shared interests, or industry-specific issues.

7. Visualise Success: Before networking events or meetings, take a moment to visualise yourself successfully engaging in conversations and making meaningful connections. Visualising positive outcomes can help boost your confidence and reduce anxiety.

8. Set Realistic Goals: Networking doesn't necessarily mean meeting every single person in the

room. Set specific and achievable goals for each networking event or situation. For example, you may aim to have three meaningful conversations, exchange contact information with two individuals, or learn something new from one person. Setting these goals can help you channel your focus, making networking less intimidating.

9. Practice Regularly: Like any skill, networking becomes easier with practice. Challenge yourself to attend events regularly, engage in conversation, and push past your comfort zone. The more you practise, the more confident and proficient you will become.

10. Seek Support from a Mentor: Finding a mentor who excels in networking can provide you with guidance and support as you overcome your fears. They can share their experiences, offer advice, and even accompany you to networking events until you feel more comfortable networking independently.

Remember, overcoming fear and shyness in networking is a gradual process. It may take time to build confidence and overcome these obstacles completely. However, by adopting a positive mindset, preparing in advance, practising active listening, attending workshops, and seeking support, you can gradually become a more confident networker. Embrace networking as an opportunity for growth and personal development, and you will find your fear and shyness diminishing over time, leading to enhanced networking skills and increased professional success.

5.2 Building Authentic Connections

One of the key aspects of successful networking is building authentic connections. While it is important to expand your network and meet new people, the quality of those connections is just as crucial. Authentic connections are built on trust, mutual respect, and genuine interest in the other person. These connections can have a significant impact on your professional growth and opportunities. Here are some strategies to help you build authentic connections:

1. Be Yourself: Authenticity starts with being true to yourself. Be genuine in your interactions and conversations. Let your personality shine through and avoid putting on a façade. People appreciate authenticity and are more likely to form a connection when they feel they are interacting with the real you.

2. Show Genuine Interest: When engaging in conversations, make an effort to show genuine interest in the other person. Listen attentively, ask thoughtful questions, and seek to understand their perspectives and experiences. This demonstrates that you value their input and creates a foundation for building a meaningful connection.

3. Find Common Ground: Look for shared interests, experiences, or values that you can bond over. Finding common ground helps establish a connection and builds rapport. It can be anything from a shared hobby or passion to similar career goals or industry experiences. Use these commonalities as conversation starters and opportunities to connect on a deeper level.

4. Be a Good Listener: Active listening is key to building authentic connections. Give the other person your undivided attention, avoid interrupting, and refrain from jumping to conclusions. Ask open-ended questions to encourage the other person to share more about themselves. By demonstrating that you are genuinely interested in what they have to say, you will establish a deeper connection.

5. Show Empathy: Empathy plays a vital role in building authentic connections. Put yourself in the other person's shoes and try to understand their

perspective. Show empathy by acknowledging their challenges, celebrating their successes, and providing support when needed. Showing empathy builds trust and strengthens the connection.

6. Be Reliable and Trustworthy: Building trust is crucial when establishing authentic connections. Keep your promises, follow through on commitments, and be reliable. If you say you will do something, make sure you deliver. Being trustworthy and dependable builds credibility and reinforces the authenticity of the connection.

7. Share Vulnerability: Authentic connections often involve a level of vulnerability. Share your own experiences, challenges, and lessons learned. By opening up and being vulnerable, you create a safe and trusting environment for others to do the same. This deeper level of sharing strengthens the connection and fosters a sense of camaraderie.

8. Be Supportive: Actively support and uplift the people in your network. Celebrate their achievements, provide encouragement during setbacks, and offer assistance when needed. By being a positive and supportive force, you create a bond that goes beyond superficial networking.

9. Follow-up and Maintain Relationships: Building authentic connections is not a one-time event; it requires ongoing effort. Follow up with the people you connect with, whether it's through email, phone calls, or meet-ups. Stay in touch and nurture the relationship over time. Remember important details about their lives and careers, and make an effort to reach out regularly. This demonstrates your genuine interest in their well-being and strengthens the connection.

10. Give without Expecting Immediate Returns: Authentic connections are built on a foundation of mutual support and generosity. Offer your assistance, share valuable resources, and connect people within your network without expecting an immediate return. By being generous and helpful, you foster goodwill and create a network of people who are invested in your success as well.

Building authentic connections requires time, effort, and genuine interest in others. By being yourself, showing genuine interest, finding common ground, and demonstrating reliability and trustworthiness, you can establish meaningful connections that will support your professional growth and contribute to your success. Remember, networking is not just about collecting business cards; it's about building relationships based on authenticity, mutual respect, and a shared desire to support one another's success.

5.3 Managing Time and Prioritising Network Building Activities

In the fast-paced world of professional networking, managing time effectively and prioritising network building activities is vital for success. Building and maintaining a strong professional network requires effort and commitment, but with proper time management techniques, it can be accomplished alongside other responsibilities. Here are strategies to help manage time and prioritise network building activities:

1. Set Clear Goals: Start by setting specific goals for your networking efforts. Identify what you hope to achieve through networking, whether it's career advancement, business opportunities, or personal development. Having clear goals will help you prioritise activities that align with your objectives.

2. Create a Networking Schedule: Dedicate specific time slots in your schedule for networking activities. Treat these slots as important appointments and commit to them consistently. By setting aside dedicated time for networking, you

ensure that it doesn't get neglected amidst other responsibilities.

3. Prioritise High-Value Connections: Not all connections are of equal importance or relevance to your goals. Identify high-value connections within your network, such as industry experts, thought leaders, or individuals with influential positions. Prioritise building and maintaining relationships with these individuals as they can have a significant impact on your professional growth.

4. Use Efficient Strategies: Identify networking strategies that provide the greatest value in the shortest amount of time. For example, attending industry conferences or events can allow you to connect with multiple professionals in a single setting. Additionally, leveraging social media platforms can help you reach a larger audience and engage with professionals beyond your immediate network.

5. Leverage Technology: Utilise technological tools to streamline networking activities and save time. Use email templates or scheduling software to automate follow-ups and reminders. Utilise mobile apps or online platforms to connect with professionals virtually, reducing the need for in-person meetings. Embrace technology as a

resource to manage your networking efforts efficiently.

6. Focus on Quality, Not Quantity: Networking is about building authentic connections, rather than accumulating a large number of superficial contacts. Prioritise quality over quantity by investing time in developing meaningful relationships with a select group of individuals who align with your goals and values.

7. Practise Efficient Communication: Make the most of your networking conversations by being concise and focused. Clearly articulate your objectives and value propositions, and actively listen to the other person's needs and interests. By communicating efficiently, you make the most of your networking interactions and optimise your time.

8. Delegate and Outsource: In some cases, it may be beneficial to delegate certain networking tasks to others or outsource them entirely. For example, you can assign a team member to attend networking events on your behalf or hire a virtual assistant to manage your scheduling and follow-ups. Delegating tasks allows you to prioritise your own time more effectively.

9. Continuously Assess and Refine: Regularly assess the effectiveness of your networking activities and adjust your approach as necessary. Evaluate which connections and strategies are yielding the desired results and prioritise accordingly. Be willing to adapt and refine your networking plan to maximise your time and efforts.

10. Be Disciplined and Consistent: Consistency is key in networking. Stay disciplined and committed to your networking schedule even when time constraints arise. By consistently investing time in building and maintaining your network, you will reap the long-term benefits of a strong professional community.

Managing time and prioritising network building activities can be a challenge, but with deliberate planning and organisation, it is possible to effectively incorporate networking into your professional life. By setting clear goals, prioritising high-value connections, leveraging efficient strategies, and utilising technology, you can optimise your time and make the most of your networking efforts. Remember, networking is an ongoing process that requires consistent dedication and attention to yield meaningful results.

5.4 Dealing with Rejection and Overcoming Setbacks

In the journey of building a professional network, it is inevitable that one may face rejection and setbacks along the way. Dealing with these challenges is crucial for maintaining motivation and continuing to grow and develop connections. Here are strategies for handling rejection and overcoming setbacks in professional networking:

1. Acceptance and Resilience: The first step in dealing with rejection is accepting that it is a normal part of the networking process. Not every connection or opportunity will work out, and that is perfectly okay. Cultivate resilience by understanding that rejection is not a reflection of your worth or abilities, but rather a natural part of any professional journey.

2. Reflect and Learn: Instead of dwelling on rejections or setbacks, take the opportunity to reflect and learn from them. Analyse the situation and look for possible areas of improvement. Consider what may have led to the rejection and how you can refine your approach or strategy moving forward. Every setback can be a valuable lesson for personal and professional growth.

3. Seek Feedback: In some cases, it may be helpful to seek feedback from those who have rejected your networking attempts. Politely ask for their perspective or advice on how you can enhance your approach. Constructive feedback can provide valuable insights and help you adjust your networking strategies for future interactions.

4. Stay Positive and Maintain Confidence: Rejection or setbacks can demotivate and undermine confidence. It is important to maintain a positive mindset and believe in your capabilities. Remind yourself of your achievements and strengths, and don't let setbacks define your self-worth. Confidence is key in networking, so continue to present yourself with poise and professionalism.

5. Build a Supportive Network: Having a supportive network can provide reassurance and encouragement during challenging times. Reach out to mentors, advisors, or trusted colleagues who can offer guidance and support. Engage in networking groups or communities where you can share experiences and learn from others who have faced similar obstacles.

6. Adapt and Refocus: Rejection and setbacks can be an opportunity to reevaluate your goals and

priorities. Consider if there are any adjustments you need to make in your networking approach. Be flexible and open to new opportunities or connections that may arise. Use setbacks as a chance to refocus and redirect your efforts towards new avenues or target connections.

7. Stay Persistent and Consistent: Perseverance is key in overcoming setbacks. Maintain your dedication to networking and stay persistent in your efforts. Don't let rejection discourage you from continuing to expand your network. Consistent and ongoing networking activities increase the likelihood of discovering new opportunities and connections.

8. Celebrate Small Wins: It's important to celebrate the small victories along the way, even amidst rejection and setbacks. Recognize and appreciate the progress you have made, whether it's successful connections, positive feedback, or any milestones achieved. Celebrating small wins boosts confidence, motivation, and resilience in the face of challenges.

9. Embrace a Growth Mindset: Adopt a growth mindset by viewing rejection and setbacks as opportunities for growth and development. Embrace the belief that with effort and perseverance, you can improve your networking skills and achieve your

goals. Emphasise learning and continuous improvement, and see setbacks as stepping stones towards success.

Dealing with rejection and overcoming setbacks is an essential part of the professional networking journey. By accepting and learning from rejections, staying positive and confident, seeking feedback, building a supportive network, adapting and refocusing, staying persistent and consistent, celebrating small wins, and embracing a growth mindset, you can navigate through setbacks and continue to build a strong and successful professional network. Remember that resilience and perseverance are key in overcoming obstacles and achieving long-term networking success.

CHAPTER 6

Enhancing Networking Skills

Networking skills are essential for building and maintaining professional connections, advancing in careers, and accessing new opportunities. Improving and enhancing these skills can significantly impact the effectiveness and success of networking efforts. Here are some strategies to enhance networking skills:

1. Effective and Engaging Conversation Techniques: Developing effective conversation skills is crucial for networking success. Practise active listening, ask open-ended questions, and show genuine interest in others' experiences and perspectives. Engage in meaningful conversations by sharing relevant insights, ideas, and experiences. Nonverbal cues, such as maintaining eye contact and displaying positive body language, can also enhance communication and connection with others.

2. Developing Active Listening Skills: Active listening is an essential skill for effective networking. Paying full attention to the person you are conversing with demonstrates respect and

genuine interest. Avoid interrupting or constantly thinking of your response while the other person is speaking. Instead, focus on understanding their perspective, summarising their points, and asking follow-up questions. Active listening builds rapport and strengthens connections.

3. Establishing and Maintaining Rapport: Establishing rapport is fundamental for building relationships in networking. Find common ground with others, such as shared interests or experiences, and use it as a starting point for conversation. Show empathy, be approachable and friendly, and maintain a positive and professional demeanour. Authenticity and creating a relaxed and comfortable atmosphere can help foster rapport and make people more comfortable networking with you.

4. Mastering the Art of Follow-up and Relationship Building: Following up after initial networking interactions is essential for relationship building and maintaining connections. Send personalised and timely follow-up messages or emails to express gratitude for the conversation and express interest in future collaborations or meetings. Stay in touch regularly through appropriate channels, such as social media platforms, email, or phone calls. Continuously nurture relationships by offering

support, sharing relevant information or resources, and engaging in meaningful conversations.

5. Expanding Networking Skills Online: In the digital age, online networking platforms play a significant role in building connections. Enhance your networking skills by mastering online platforms such as LinkedIn, Twitter, or industry-specific forums. Utilise these platforms to connect with professionals in your field, join relevant groups or communities, and share valuable insights and resources. Engage in discussions, participate in webinars or virtual events, and leverage the power of online networking to expand your reach and connect with a diverse range of professionals.

6. Developing Confidence and Overcoming Shyness: Building confidence is crucial for effective networking. If shyness or social anxiety hinders networking efforts, practice stepping out of your comfort zone gradually. Attend small networking events, join supportive networking groups, or engage in activities that boost self-esteem. Positive affirmations, visualisation exercises, and seeking opportunities for public speaking or presenting can help in building confidence and overcoming shyness.

7. Continuous Learning: Networking skills are not innate but can be developed and honed through continuous learning. Seek out opportunities for professional development or networking training to improve and refine your skills. Attend workshops, seminars, or conferences that focus on networking strategies or interpersonal communication. Read books or listen to podcasts on networking and relationship building to gain new insights and perspectives. Learning from others' experiences and expertise can help strengthen networking skills.

8. Seeking Feedback and Self-Reflection: Actively seek feedback from trusted peers, mentors, or networking partners to understand how you can enhance your networking skills. Ask for their observations and suggestions for improvement. Additionally, engage in self-reflection to identify areas where you can grow. Analyse your networking experiences, consider what worked well and what can be improved, and make adjustments accordingly.

By consistently practising and enhancing these networking skills, you can become a more confident and effective networker. Building strong connections, fostering meaningful relationships, and accessing new opportunities become more attainable as you continue to refine and enhance your networking skills. Remember, networking is not just about collecting business cards—it's about cultivating genuine relationships and mutually beneficial connections.

6. Enhancing Networking Skills

Networking is more than just exchanging business cards or connecting on social media. To truly excel at networking and build strong connections, professionals need to enhance their networking skills. In this section, we will explore some key techniques and strategies for enhancing networking skills that will help individuals become more effective and engaging networkers.

6.1 Effective and Engaging Conversation Techniques

One of the most important networking skills is the ability to engage in effective and engaging conversations. Networking events and conferences often provide opportunities for professionals to meet new people and make valuable connections. However, many individuals find themselves at a loss when it comes to starting and maintaining conversations.

To enhance conversation skills in networking situations, it is crucial to have a clear understanding of the purpose of networking. Networking is about building relationships and establishing connections, so it is important to approach conversations with genuine interest and curiosity.

Here are some techniques to help improve conversation skills:

1. Be prepared: Before attending a networking event, research the attendees and the topics that will be discussed. This will help you have something meaningful to talk about and show that you are knowledgeable and interested in the industry or field.

2. Have a memorable introduction: Craft an engaging and concise introduction that highlights your expertise or unique selling points. This will help you make a strong first impression and capture the attention of the person you are speaking to.

3. Ask open-ended questions: Open-ended questions encourage conversation and provide opportunities for the other person to share their thoughts and experiences. This helps to create a more interactive and engaging discussion.

4. Practise active listening: Give the person you are speaking to your full attention and actively listen to what they are saying. This means not interrupting, maintaining eye contact, and using verbal and non-verbal cues to show that you are engaged in the conversation.

5. Show genuine interest: Show a genuine interest in the other person's work and accomplishments. Ask follow-up questions and seek to understand their perspective. This demonstrates that you value their insights and establishes a foundation for a meaningful connection.

6. Be mindful of body language: Your body language plays a significant role in how you are perceived during networking conversations. Maintain good posture, make open and welcoming gestures, and smile to create a positive and approachable impression.

7. Share information and resources: Networking is a two-way street, so be willing to share your knowledge, expertise, and resources with others. This not only builds goodwill but also establishes you as a valuable contact in the eyes of others.

8. Practice self-confidence: Confidence is key when it comes to networking. Believe in yourself and

your abilities, and approach conversations with a positive attitude. This will make you more approachable and memorable to others.

By incorporating these conversation techniques into networking interactions, professionals can become more effective communicators and build genuine connections with others. Effective conversation skills not only help in networking situations but also in various professional scenarios, such as meetings, presentations, and interviews. Constant practice and feedback from others can further enhance these skills and make networking a more comfortable and rewarding experience.

Enhancing conversation techniques is a crucial aspect of improving networking skills. By being prepared, practising active listening, showing genuine interest, and maintaining positive body language, professionals can become more effective and engaging networkers. These skills not only help build meaningful connections but also contribute to overall professional success.

6.2 Developing Active Listening Skills

Active listening is a critical skill in any form of communication, and it plays a significant role in networking. When engaging in networking conversations, actively listening to the other person demonstrates respect, interest, and a willingness to understand their perspective. This skill not only helps build stronger connections but also allows professionals to gather valuable information and insights that can be utilised in their careers.

Developing active listening skills involves a combination of techniques and mindset shifts. Here are some strategies to enhance active listening in networking:

1. Eliminate distractions: When engaging in a networking conversation, remove any distractions that might hinder active listening. Put away your phone, close any open screens, and focus your attention solely on the person speaking.

2. Maintain eye contact: Eye contact is a powerful non-verbal cue that shows you are fully present and engaged in the conversation. It conveys respect and helps establish a connection with the other person.

3. Practise non-verbal cues: In addition to eye contact, other non-verbal cues such as nodding, smiling, and leaning in slightly can signal to the speaker that you are actively listening. These cues

demonstrate your interest and encourage the speaker to continue sharing.

4. Avoid interrupting: Giving the speaker the space to express themselves without interruption is crucial for effective active listening. Allow them to finish their thoughts before interjecting with your own perspective or questions.

5. Ask probing questions: Asking thoughtful and open-ended questions shows that you are actively engaged in the conversation and interested in learning more. These questions can help uncover additional insights and allow the speaker to delve deeper into their ideas.

6. Paraphrase and summarise: Throughout the conversation, periodically paraphrase or summarise the speaker's main points to ensure your understanding and demonstrate that you are actively processing the information. This also provides an opportunity for clarification if needed.

7. Practice empathy: Active listening involves putting yourself in the speaker's shoes and seeking to understand their perspective. Show genuine empathy and validate their feelings, experiences, and challenges.

8. Avoid distractions in your mind: Maintain focus on the speaker's words and avoid allowing your mind to wander. Be fully present and resist the temptation to plan your response or think about other things while the person is speaking.

Developing active listening skills takes practice and conscious effort. It requires a commitment to being fully present and engaged in conversations, as well as a genuine curiosity about others. Active listening not only helps build stronger connections by making the other person feel heard and understood, but it also allows you to gather valuable insights and information that can be beneficial in your professional life.

By honing active listening skills, professionals can create a positive and mutually beneficial networking experience. They will be able to forge deeper connections, gain a better understanding of their industry, learn from others' experiences, and establish themselves as trustworthy and valued networkers. Active listening is a skill that can be applied not only in networking but also in various professional and personal contexts, making it an essential tool for success.

6.3 Establishing and Maintaining Rapport

Building rapport is essential in networking because it lays the foundation for a strong and mutually beneficial relationship. Rapport refers to the sense of connection, trust, and understanding that is established between individuals. When networking, establishing rapport helps create a comfortable and positive environment for both parties, leading to more meaningful and productive interactions.

To establish and maintain rapport in networking, consider the following strategies:

1. Be genuine and authentic: Authenticity is key to building rapport. Be true to yourself and present your genuine self when engaging with others. People can sense when someone is being insincere, so it's important to be authentic in your interactions.

2. Find common ground: Look for common interests, experiences, or goals that you share with the person you are networking with. This can help establish a sense of connection and rapport right from the start. Discussing shared interests or experiences can create a comfortable atmosphere and help you establish a bond.

3. Show interest and listen actively: Demonstrate genuine interest in the other person by actively listening to what they have to say. Show curiosity and ask open-ended questions to encourage them to share more about their experiences and perspectives. By listening actively, you not only build rapport but also gain valuable insights and information.

4. Use positive body language: Non-verbal cues play a significant role in building rapport. Maintain good eye contact, use open and welcoming body language, and smile genuinely. These gestures help create a positive atmosphere and establish a connection with the other person.

5. Mirror and match communication style: People tend to feel more comfortable around those who share similar communication styles. Observe the other person's tone of voice, pace of speech, and body language, and adapt your own communication style to match theirs. This can help create a sense of harmony and understanding.

6. Show empathy and understanding: Empathy is crucial in establishing rapport. Show understanding and empathy towards the other person's challenges, perspectives, and experiences. Validate their feelings and offer support if appropriate. This

demonstrates that you are invested in their success and fosters a sense of trust and rapport.

7. Follow up and maintain regular communication: After the initial networking interaction, follow up with the person to express your appreciation for their time and continue building the relationship. Regularly staying in touch through emails, phone calls, or meetings helps maintain rapport and keeps the connection alive.

8. Provide value and support: Rapport is not just about taking; it's also about giving. Look for ways to provide value to the other person, such as sharing relevant resources, recommending them for opportunities, or offering assistance. By being supportive and helpful, you strengthen the rapport and create a positive impression.

Building and maintaining rapport in networking takes time and effort. It requires active engagement, listening, and a genuine interest in others. By establishing rapport, professionals can create a foundation for long-lasting and mutually beneficial relationships. Rapport helps to build trust, allows for open communication, and ultimately paves the way for collaboration and professional growth.

6.4 Mastering the Art of Follow-up and Relationship Building

Follow-up and relationship building are crucial aspects of networking that lead to long-lasting and fruitful connections. While initiating contact and establishing rapport are important, it's equally important to maintain and nurture those relationships over time. Mastering the art of follow-up and relationship building can significantly enhance networking effectiveness and create opportunities for professional growth.

To master the art of follow-up and relationship building, consider the following strategies:

1. Promptly follow up after initial meetings: After meeting someone at a networking event or conference, promptly follow up within a few days to express your gratitude for their time and reiterate your interest in staying connected. This shows professionalism and leaves a positive impression.

2. Personalise your follow-up: When following up, tailor your message to the individual and refer to specific points or conversations from your initial meeting. This personal touch demonstrates your attentiveness and makes the recipient feel valued and remembered.

3. Provide value in your communications: Offer resources, insights, or connections that could benefit the other person. By providing value, you establish yourself as a valuable contact and increase the chances of the relationship becoming mutually beneficial.

4. Maintain regular communication: Keep in touch with your network on a regular basis. Share relevant articles, industry updates, or information that may be of interest to them. This helps to nurture the relationship and reinforces your commitment to staying connected.

5. Use a variety of communication channels: Utilise different communication channels, such as email, phone calls, social media, or in-person meetings, to connect with your network. Consider the preferences of your contacts and adapt your approach accordingly.

6. Remember important dates or milestones: Take note of important dates in your network's lives, such as birthdays, work anniversaries, or promotions, and reach out to acknowledge and celebrate these occasions. This thoughtful gesture shows that you value the person and strengthens the relationship.

7. Actively engage with your network's content: Like, comment, and share the content shared by your network on social media platforms. Interacting with their content shows support and helps to maintain visibility and engagement within your network.

8. Leverage technology and automation: Use customer relationship management (CRM) software or email automation tools to streamline your follow-up process. These tools can help you stay organised, schedule reminders, and personalise your communications at scale.

9. Seek opportunities for face-to-face interactions: While technology allows for convenient communication, in-person meetings are invaluable for deepening relationships. Whenever possible, arrange coffee meetings, lunches, or attend industry events together. Face-to-face interactions provide a more personal and memorable experience.

10. Show gratitude and reciprocate favours: When someone in your network provides assistance or support, express genuine gratitude. Be willing to reciprocate favours when the opportunity arises, as this helps to strengthen the bond and create a sense of reciprocity within the relationship.

By mastering the art of follow-up and relationship building, professionals can turn initial connections into powerful and mutually beneficial alliances. Cultivating relationships through consistent communication, providing value, and showing genuine interest helps to establish trust and credibility. These relationships can lead to valuable opportunities, referrals, collaborations, and personal growth. Therefore, investing time and effort into maintaining and nurturing your professional network is essential for long-term success.

CHAPTER 7

Cultivating a Network of Resources

Building a strong network of resources is crucial for professional success. A network of resources consists of individuals, organisations, and tools that can provide valuable information, support, and opportunities. Cultivating such a network allows professionals to tap into a wealth of knowledge, expertise, and connections that can enhance their work, expand their reach, and open doors to new possibilities. Here are some strategies for effectively cultivating a network of resources:

1. Identify your needs: Before cultivating a network of resources, it's essential to identify your specific needs and goals. Determine what kind of resources would be most helpful to you in your professional journey. This could include industry experts, mentors, professional development programs, online platforms, or industry-specific tools and software.

2. Attend industry events and conferences: Industry events and conferences provide a valuable opportunity to meet and connect with other

professionals in your field. Take the time to engage in meaningful conversations, ask questions, and exchange contact information. Follow up with those you meet to continue building the relationship and leverage their expertise and insights when needed.

3. Join professional associations and organisations: Professional associations and organisations provide a platform for networking with like-minded individuals in your industry. These groups often offer conferences, webinars, workshops, and other events where you can learn from experienced professionals and build relationships. Take an active role within these organisations by volunteering, serving on committees, or joining leadership positions to expand your network even further.

4. Seek out mentors and advisors: Mentors and advisors can provide valuable guidance and support throughout your professional journey. Look for individuals who possess the expertise and experience you admire and reach out to them. Building a strong relationship with a mentor or advisor can open doors to new opportunities, provide valuable insights, and help you navigate challenges effectively.

5. Leverage online platforms: Online platforms, such as LinkedIn and professional forums, offer

opportunities to connect with professionals worldwide. Actively engage in relevant discussions, share your expertise, and reach out to individuals who can contribute to your network of resources. Join online communities and groups specific to your industry or interests to connect with individuals who share similar goals and challenges.

6. Cultivate relationships with industry experts and thought leaders: Identify and connect with thought leaders and experts in your field. Follow their work, attend their presentations or webinars, and engage in conversations with them. Building relationships with industry influencers can provide you with access to valuable information, opportunities, and connections that can contribute to your professional growth.

7. Establish collaborative partnerships: Seek out collaborative partnerships with individuals, organisations, or businesses whose skills and resources complement your own. Cultivating collaborative relationships can expand your network, enhance your offerings, and create mutually beneficial opportunities for growth and success.

8. Offer your resources and expertise: Cultivating a network of resources is not just about receiving. It's

equally important to offer your own resources and expertise to others. Share your knowledge, provide assistance, and be proactive in helping others in your network. By being generous with your resources, you build trust and strengthen your relationships.

9. Maintain and nurture your network: Building a network of resources is an ongoing process. Regularly engage with your network by attending events, connecting on social media, and reaching out for updates or conversations. Stay updated on their work and achievements, and stay in touch with them through regular communication. Remember, relationships require effort and nurturing to thrive.

10. Pay it forward: As you cultivate a network of resources and benefit from the support you receive, consider paying it forward. Be open to helping others who reach out to you for guidance or assistance. By sharing your resources and expertise with others, you contribute to the growth and success of your broader professional community.

Cultivating a network of resources is a strategic investment that can significantly enhance your professional journey. By connecting with individuals, organisations, and tools that offer valuable resources, you can gain insights, opportunities, and support that can propel your career forward. Remember, cultivating and maintaining a strong network requires time, effort, and genuine relationships built on trust and mutual respect.

7.1 Building a Network of Industry Experts and Thought Leaders

One of the key components of a successful professional network is having access to industry experts and thought leaders. Building relationships with these individuals can provide invaluable insights, guidance, and opportunities for growth and development. Here are some strategies for effectively building a network of industry experts and thought leaders:

1. Identify the experts: Start by identifying key industry experts and thought leaders in your field. These individuals are typically recognized for their expertise and contributions to the industry. Research industry publications, online forums, conferences, and events to identify the prominent voices in your field.

2. Follow their work: Once you have identified the experts, follow their work closely. This can include

reading their articles, books, or blogs, watching their presentations or videos, or listening to their podcasts or interviews. By staying updated on their work, you will have a deeper understanding of their perspectives and insights.

3. Engage in conversations: Engage with industry experts and thought leaders through various channels such as social media, online communities, or industry-specific forums. Participate in discussions, ask questions, and share your thoughts or experiences. Actively engage in these conversations to demonstrate your knowledge and interest in the industry.

4. Attend industry events: Industry events such as conferences, seminars, or workshops provide an excellent opportunity to connect with industry experts and thought leaders. Attend their sessions, introduce yourself, and ask relevant questions during Q&A sessions. Networking events held as part of these conferences also provide a more informal setting to interact with these experts.

5. Seek out mentorship opportunities: Building a mentor-mentee relationship with an industry expert or thought leader can provide valuable guidance and support. Reach out to individuals whose work you admire and explain why you would benefit from

their mentorship. Be polite, genuine, and sincere in your approach, and demonstrate your eagerness to learn from them.

6. Provide value: When connecting with industry experts and thought leaders, it's important to offer value in return. Share your own insights, research, or experiences that may be relevant to their work. Offer to collaborate on projects, contribute articles, or provide assistance in areas where you excel. By providing value, you can establish yourself as a valuable connection in their network.

7. Build genuine relationships: Networking is not just about collecting business cards or LinkedIn connections; it's about building genuine relationships. Take the time to understand the person behind the industry expertise. Show genuine interest in their work, ask about their experiences, and find common ground. Building a genuine relationship based on mutual respect and shared interests will strengthen the connection over time.

8. Stay in touch: Once you have established a connection with industry experts and thought leaders, it's important to maintain regular contact. Send periodic updates, share relevant articles or resources, or invite them to industry events or webinars you are involved in. Cultivate the

relationship by demonstrating your ongoing interest and keeping them informed about your own professional development.

Building a network of industry experts and thought leaders can significantly enhance your professional journey. These individuals can provide valuable insights, guidance, and opportunities that may not be available through other channels. Moreover, being connected to these influential individuals can enhance your professional credibility and reputation within your industry. Remember, building and maintaining these relationships requires time, effort, and genuine interest in their work.

7.2 Establishing Collaborative Partnerships

Networking is not just about building connections with individuals, but also about establishing collaborative partnerships with other professionals and organisations. Collaborations can help you leverage complementary strengths and resources, expand your reach, and achieve mutually beneficial goals. Here are some strategies for establishing collaborative partnerships:

1. Identify potential partners: Identify individuals, businesses, or organisations that align with your goals and values. Look for those who have expertise or resources that can complement your own. Consider both within your industry and in related fields, as diverse partnerships can bring fresh perspectives and opportunities.

2. Research and evaluate: Research potential partners thoroughly. Review their work, reputation, values, and past collaborations. Look for evidence of compatibility and shared objectives. Determine whether the potential partner's strengths and offerings can add value to your own work or enhance your products and services.

3. Reach out with a tailored proposal: When approaching potential partners, craft a compelling proposal that outlines the potential benefits of collaboration and how it aligns with their goals. Personalise your outreach, demonstrating that you have done your research and have identified specific ways in which collaboration can be mutually beneficial. Clearly express how you envision working together and what you bring to the partnership.

4. Foster trust and transparency: Building trust is crucial for successful collaborations. Be transparent

about your own goals, capabilities, and limitations. Communicate openly and honestly with potential partners about what you can offer and what you expect in return. Address any concerns or potential challenges upfront, and be receptive to feedback and suggestions from the other party.

5. Define shared goals and expectations: Collaborations thrive on clear and mutually agreed-upon goals and expectations. Take the time to define these with your partners, ensuring that everyone is on the same page. Establish key milestones, responsibilities, and timelines. Regularly communicate progress and address any issues that arise promptly.

6. Promote a win-win mindset: Focus on creating value for both yourself and your partners. Look for ways to contribute equitably to the collaboration and seek opportunities for shared success. Maintain open lines of communication and seek feedback throughout the partnership to ensure that both parties' interests are acknowledged and addressed.

7. Leverage each other's networks: Collaborative partnerships offer an opportunity to access new networks and expand your reach. Encourage your partners to introduce you to their contacts and vice versa. Jointly promote each other's work, products,

or services through cross-marketing initiatives. Leveraging each other's networks can lead to increased visibility and potential business opportunities.

8. Regularly evaluate and adjust: Regularly assess the progress of your collaborative partnerships. Evaluate whether the expected benefits and outcomes are being realised and if the partnership is still aligned with your goals. If necessary, be open to adjusting or renegotiating aspects of the collaboration to ensure its continued relevance and effectiveness.

Establishing collaborative partnerships can open doors to new opportunities, diversify your offerings, and help you achieve goals that may be difficult to accomplish alone. By pooling resources, knowledge, and networks, you can create synergies that lead to mutual growth and success. Remember, successful partnerships require trust, effective communication, shared goals, and continuous evaluation and adjustment.

7.3 Leveraging Your Network for Professional Opportunities

Building a professional network is not just about making connections for the sake of it. It's about leveraging those connections to create and access opportunities that can propel your career or business forward. Your network can serve as a valuable resource for finding new clients, job opportunities, partnerships, mentorship, and much more. Here are some strategies for leveraging your network for professional opportunities:

1. Clearly define your goals: Before you start reaching out to your network for opportunities, it's essential to clearly define your goals. What specific opportunities are you seeking? Are you looking for new clients, job opportunities, collaboration opportunities, or something else? Having a clear understanding of what you're looking for will help you effectively communicate your needs to your network.

2. Communicate your intentions: Once you have defined your goals, communicate them to your network. Let them know what types of opportunities you are interested in and how they can help you. Be specific and concise in your requests so that others

can easily understand what you need and can provide appropriate support.

3. Develop a targeted approach: Instead of randomly reaching out to everyone in your network, develop a targeted approach. Identify individuals or groups within your network who are most likely to have the connections or resources you need. Reach out to them directly and explain why you think they might be able to help you. Personalise your requests to show that you value their specific expertise and insights.

4. Offer value in return: Networking is a two-way street, and it's important to offer value in return for the opportunities you seek. Consider how you can help others in your network and be proactive in offering your assistance. By providing value to others, you build goodwill and increase the likelihood of them wanting to help you and support your goals.

5. Follow up and stay connected: Building and nurturing relationships is key to leveraging your network for opportunities. Follow up with individuals in your network regularly to maintain a strong connection. Keep them updated on your progress, share relevant information or resources, and genuinely show interest in their endeavours.

The stronger your relationships, the more likely others will think of you when opportunities arise.

6. Attend industry events and conferences: Industry events and conferences provide excellent opportunities for networking and accessing new professional opportunities. Attend these events and make an effort to connect with fellow attendees, speakers, and sponsors. Actively engage in conversations and follow up afterward to deepen relationships and explore potential collaborations or job prospects.

7. Utilise online platforms: Leverage online platforms, such as LinkedIn, to expand your network and discover new opportunities. Join relevant professional groups and actively participate in discussions. Share valuable content and insights to position yourself as an industry expert and attract opportunities. Use the platform to connect with individuals in your target industries or companies and explore potential collaborations or job openings.

8. Be proactive in seeking referrals: Don't be afraid to ask for referrals from your network. If you're seeking a job, ask for introductions to hiring managers or HR professionals who might have relevant openings. If you're looking for clients, ask

for recommendations or referrals to individuals or businesses in need of your services. Your network can open doors you may not have access to otherwise.

Remember, leveraging your network for professional opportunities requires active engagement and relationship-building. It's not enough to simply have connections. You must nurture those relationships, offer value, and proactively communicate your needs and goals. By effectively leveraging your network, you can tap into a wide range of opportunities that can propel your career or business to new heights.

7.4 Creating a Supportive Network for Personal and Professional Growth

Building a strong professional network is not just about accessing opportunities and advancing your career or business. It's also about creating a supportive community that can contribute to your personal and professional growth. A supportive network can provide guidance, motivation, and encouragement during challenging times. Here are some strategies for creating a supportive network for personal and professional growth:

1. Surround yourself with positive and like-minded individuals: Seek out individuals who have a positive mindset and share similar goals and values. Surrounding yourself with like-minded individuals creates a supportive environment where you can motivate and inspire each other. Positive and supportive individuals can also help you maintain a resilient mindset and overcome obstacles.

2. Find mentors and advisors: Mentors and advisors play a crucial role in personal and professional growth. Look for individuals who have expertise and experience in your desired field or industry. They can provide guidance, share valuable insights, and offer advice based on their own experiences. Regular conversations and interactions with mentors can help you gain new perspectives, develop new skills, and make informed decisions.

3. Participate in mastermind groups: Joining mastermind groups can be highly beneficial for personal and professional growth. Mastermind groups consist of individuals with diverse skills and backgrounds who come together to support and challenge each other. These groups provide a safe and confidential space for brainstorming ideas, seeking feedback, and sharing knowledge. Being part of a mastermind group can help you gain fresh

perspectives, expand your network, and accelerate your growth.

4. Offer support and reciprocity: Building a supportive network is a two-way street. Just as you seek support from others, offer your support and assistance whenever possible. Be genuinely interested in the success and well-being of others in your network. Celebrate their achievements, offer your help when they face challenges, and be a source of motivation and encouragement. By being supportive to others, you cultivate a reciprocal environment where others are more likely to support your growth as well.

5. Attend personal development workshops and seminars: Personal development workshops and seminars provide valuable opportunities for growth and self-improvement. They allow you to learn new skills, gain insights from experts, and connect with like-minded individuals. Engaging in personal development activities not only enhances your knowledge and skills but also exposes you to new perspectives and ideas that can contribute to your personal and professional growth.

6. Foster a culture of collaboration and sharing: Encourage collaboration and knowledge sharing within your network. Share your expertise,

resources, and connections with others who can benefit from it. Actively participate in discussions, contribute meaningful insights, and offer help whenever possible. By fostering a culture of collaboration and sharing, you create an environment where individuals can learn and grow together.

7. Regularly evaluate and nurture your network: Periodically assess the members of your network to ensure they align with your goals and values. Identify individuals who provide meaningful support and contribute to your growth. Nurture those relationships by staying in regular contact, offering assistance, and expressing genuine appreciation for their support. On the other hand, take steps to distance yourself from negative or toxic relationships that hinder your growth or drain your energy.

Creating a supportive network for personal and professional growth requires intentional effort and genuine connections. By surrounding yourself with positive and like-minded individuals, finding mentors and advisors, participating in mastermind groups, offering support, attending personal development activities, fostering collaboration, and regularly evaluating and nurturing your network, you can create a supportive environment that accelerates your growth and success.

CHAPTER 8

Networking Etiquette and Best Practices

Networking can be a powerful tool for building professional relationships and advancing your career or business. However, it's important to approach networking with the right etiquette and adhere to best practices to ensure that your interactions are effective and impactful. Here are some guidelines for networking etiquette and best practices:

1. Be genuine and authentic: One of the most important aspects of networking is being genuine and authentic in your interactions. People can easily detect insincerity, so it's crucial to approach networking with a genuine interest in others and their work. Avoid being overly self-promotional or transactional in your conversations. Instead, focus on building meaningful connections based on shared interests or goals.

2. Listen actively: Effective networking involves active listening. When engaging in conversations, make an effort to listen attentively to what the other

person is saying. Show genuine interest by asking thoughtful questions and seeking to understand their experiences, challenges, and goals. Active listening not only creates a stronger connection but also allows you to gather valuable insights that can inform how you can provide support or add value.

3. Practise effective communication: Good communication skills are essential in networking. Clearly articulate your ideas, thoughts, and goals in a concise and confident manner. Be mindful of your tone, body language, and non-verbal cues to ensure your message is conveyed effectively. When communicating online, be mindful of your written communication and always strive for professionalism and clarity.

4. Respect boundaries and privacy: While networking involves building relationships, it's important to respect personal boundaries and privacy. Avoid prying into personal matters or asking intrusive questions. If someone indicates discomfort or hesitancy in discussing certain topics, gracefully move on to another subject. Similarly, be mindful of sharing confidential or sensitive information unless it is appropriate and mutually beneficial for the relationship.

5. Follow up promptly: After a networking interaction, it's essential to follow up promptly to maintain the momentum and show your gratitude and interest. Send a personalised thank-you note or email expressing appreciation for the conversation and any insights or advice shared. If appropriate, mention any action steps you plan to take based on the discussion. Following up not only helps solidify the connection but also leaves a positive impression.

6. Cultivate a diverse network: Networking is not just about connecting with individuals who are similar to you. It's important to proactively seek out diverse perspectives and experiences. A diverse network can provide unique insights, challenge your assumptions, and open doors to new opportunities. Engaging with individuals from different industries, cultures, and backgrounds can broaden your horizons and help you develop a more inclusive and well-rounded perspective.

7. Practice reciprocity: Networking is a two-way street, and it's important to offer support and assistance to others in your network. Be willing to share your knowledge, resources, and connections whenever possible. Offer to help others in their endeavours, provide introductions, or share relevant opportunities. By practising reciprocity, you

contribute to a supportive and collaborative network where everyone benefits from each other's success.

8. Maintain professionalism: Networking is a professional activity, so it's crucial to maintain a high level of professionalism in all interactions. Dress appropriately for networking events, maintain good hygiene, and be mindful of your behaviour and language. Avoid controversial or divisive topics unless it's relevant to the conversation and handled tactfully. Respond to communication in a timely manner and be reliable in delivering on any commitments you make.

9. Be mindful of time and space: When attending networking events or conferences, be mindful of time and space. Respect others' time by being punctual and avoiding monopolising conversations. If someone seems busy or engaged in a discussion, it's best to approach them later rather than interrupting. Be aware of personal space and avoid invading someone's personal bubble or making them uncomfortable.

10. Continuously cultivate your network: Networking is an ongoing process, so it is important to continuously cultivate and expand your network. Regularly attend events, participate in industry groups, and engage in online networking platforms

to stay connected and informed. Set aside time to nurture existing relationships and seek opportunities to meet new individuals who can contribute to your professional growth.

Networking etiquette and best practices are crucial for building and maintaining strong professional relationships. By being genuine, practising active listening, communicating effectively, respecting boundaries and privacy, following up promptly, cultivating a diverse network, practising reciprocity, maintaining professionalism, being mindful of time and space, and continuously cultivating your network, you can create meaningful connections that can support your personal and professional growth.

8.1 Understanding Professional Networking Etiquette

Networking etiquette plays a crucial role in building and maintaining successful professional relationships. When engaging in networking activities, it is essential to adhere to certain etiquette guidelines to ensure that your interactions are respected, professional, and fruitful. Understanding and practising professional networking etiquette can significantly impact the effectiveness of your networking efforts.

Firstly, it is important to approach networking with a genuine and authentic mindset. Networking is about building mutually beneficial connections, so avoid being transactional or solely focused on personal gain. Instead, genuinely aim to learn from others, understand their perspectives, and foster meaningful relationships.

Always make a positive first impression by presenting yourself professionally. Dress appropriately for networking events and maintain good hygiene. When attending virtual networking sessions or using online platforms, ensure your profile and communication reflect your professionalism. Avoid using inappropriate language or unprofessional behaviour that may damage your reputation.

Active listening is a crucial component of effective networking etiquette. Show genuine interest in others and actively listen to what they have to say. Avoid interrupting, and instead, ask relevant questions that demonstrate your engagement and understanding. By actively listening, you convey respect and convey genuine interest in the individuals you are networking with.

When engaging in conversations, be mindful of the flow and dynamics. Avoid dominating the conversation or solely focusing on yourself. Networking is a two-way street, so give others an opportunity to share their thoughts and experiences. Show empathy and support by acknowledging their challenges, achievements, and perspectives. This demonstrates that you value their input and solidifies the connection.

Another important aspect of networking etiquette is respecting boundaries and privacy. Avoid prying into personal matters or asking overly personal questions, especially with individuals you have just met. Some topics, such as politics or religion, can be sensitive and divisive. It is wise to steer clear of these unless there is a shared interest or it is directly relevant to the conversation.

Promptly follow up after networking interactions to express your gratitude and maintain the momentum. Send personalised thank-you notes or emails to show your appreciation for their time and insights. If there were any action steps discussed, mention them in your follow-up, reinforcing your commitment to the connection. Timely follow-up demonstrates professionalism and cultivates a positive impression.

Maintaining professionalism in all networking interactions is vital. Be mindful of your behaviour, language, and tone. Avoid controversial or offensive topics, maintain a positive attitude, and treat everyone respectfully, regardless of their position or background. Demonstrating professionalism helps establish your reputation as a reliable and trustworthy professional.

When networking online, adhere to online etiquette as well. Be mindful of your written communication, including grammar, punctuation, and tone. Avoid using excessive abbreviations or slang that may be misunderstood or seen as unprofessional. Practise good netiquette by refraining from spamming or bombarding others with unsolicited messages.

Finally, always be mindful of time and space. Respect others' time by being punctual to networking events or virtual meetings. Avoid monopolising conversations or overstaying your welcome in a particular conversation. Be aware of personal space and boundaries, ensuring you do not make others feel uncomfortable.

By understanding and adhering to professional networking etiquette, you can build strong and positive relationships that can lead to valuable opportunities and personal growth. Effective networking etiquette fosters trust, respect, and authentic connections, enabling you to leverage your network for success.

8.2 Networking Do's and Don'ts

Networking is a powerful tool for building professional connections and advancing one's career. However, it is important to approach networking with the right mindset and follow certain guidelines to ensure success. In this section, we will explore some do's and don'ts of networking to help you navigate this essential practice effectively.

Do's:

1. Be prepared: Before attending networking events or engaging in networking activities, do your research. Familiarise yourself with the event or organisation hosting the networking opportunity and identify individuals you would like to connect with. Prepare talking points and questions that will help you start meaningful conversations.

2. Be genuine and authentic: Authenticity is key to building meaningful connections. Be yourself and show a genuine interest in others. Listen actively

and ask thoughtful questions to demonstrate your engagement. People appreciate authenticity and are more likely to remember and trust you.

3. Be proactive: Take the initiative to introduce yourself and start conversations. Approach networking with an open mindset and be willing to learn from others. Look for opportunities to help and support others, as this can lead to valuable relationships in the future.

4. Follow up: After networking interactions, make it a priority to follow up with the individuals you connected with. Send personalised thank-you emails or messages expressing your gratitude for their time and insights. Mention specific points from your conversation to demonstrate that you were attentive and valued the interaction.

5. Offer value: Networking is about creating mutually beneficial relationships. Look for opportunities to offer your knowledge, skills, or resources to others. Sharing expertise, making introductions, or providing assistance can strengthen your connections and contribute to your professional reputation.

Don'ts:

1. Don't be too self-centred: Networking is not solely about promoting yourself or your achievements. Avoid dominating conversations or constantly talking about yourself. Instead, focus on building a rapport and showing genuine interest in others. Provide value through active listening and engaging in meaningful discussions.

2. Don't be passive: Waiting for others to approach you can limit your networking opportunities. Take the initiative to introduce yourself and engage in conversations. Be proactive in seeking out networking events and activities. Remember, networking is a proactive process, and the more effort you put in, the more opportunities you will create.

3. Don't push for immediate benefits: Building strong relationships takes time, so avoid pushing for immediate favours or seeking only short-term gains. Networking is about cultivating long-term connections and fostering mutually beneficial relationships. Focus on developing trust and rapport first before expecting any favours or opportunities.

4. Don't neglect follow-up: Following up is crucial in maintaining the momentum of networking interactions. Neglecting to follow up can give the impression that you are not interested or serious

about building a relationship. Make it a habit to promptly send thank-you messages and continue the conversation by offering assistance or sharing relevant resources.

5. Don't disregard diverse perspectives and backgrounds: Embrace diversity in your networking efforts. Don't limit yourself to connecting with individuals who have similar backgrounds or interests. Engage with people from diverse industries, backgrounds, and perspectives. This can expand your knowledge and open doors to new opportunities.

By following these do's and avoiding the don'ts, you can effectively navigate networking situations and build strong professional connections. Remember that networking is a continuous process that requires patience, genuine engagement, and a willingness to offer support to others. With the right approach, networking can propel your career to new heights by providing access to valuable opportunities, insights, and resources.

8.3 Effective Networking Communication: In Person and Online

Networking is not just about attending events and collecting business cards; effective communication plays a crucial role in building and maintaining professional connections. Whether in person or online, the way you communicate can impact how others perceive you and the success of your networking efforts. In this section, we will explore effective networking communication strategies for both in-person and online interactions.

In-Person Networking Communication:

1. Introduce yourself confidently: When meeting someone for the first time, make a strong impression by introducing yourself confidently. Maintain eye contact, offer a firm handshake, and speak clearly. State your name and provide a brief overview of your professional background or current role.

2. Be concise and focused: In networking events or conferences, conversations can be brief due to time constraints. Therefore, it is essential to communicate concisely and stay focused on the key points. Prepare an elevator pitch that highlights your skills, experience, and goals. This way, you can

effectively communicate your value proposition within a short timeframe.

3. Active listening: Actively listen and engage in conversations with others. Show interest by asking open-ended questions and allowing the other person to speak. Be present in the conversation and avoid distractions. By actively listening, you demonstrate that you value others' insights and opinions.

4. Demonstrate genuine interest and empathy: Show genuine interest in the person you are speaking with. Ask insightful questions about their career, projects, or experiences. Empathise with their challenges or successes and provide support or suggestions if appropriate. Building rapport through genuine interest and empathy can help establish a strong foundation for a lasting professional relationship.

Online Networking Communication:
1. Engage with meaningful content: Engaging with others on social media platforms and online forums can be an effective way to network. Comment on posts, share valuable articles, and contribute to discussions related to your industry. By consistently adding value to the online community, you can attract the attention of like-minded professionals and expand your network.

2. Craft a compelling online profile: Your online profile should accurately represent your professional brand and highlight your skills and expertise. Use a professional photo, write a concise and engaging summary, and include relevant keywords for searchability. Keep your profile updated with your latest accomplishments and projects to attract the right connections.

3. Personalise your messages: When reaching out to individuals online, make your messages personalised and tailored to the recipient. Avoid generic connection requests or messages that lack personalization. Referencing specific shared interests or mentioning a recent article they wrote can demonstrate your genuine interest and increase the likelihood of a positive response.

4. Maintain professionalism: Online platforms can sometimes blur the line between personal and professional communication. Maintain a professional tone and ensure that your online conversations and posts reflect the image you want to project. Avoid controversial topics or engaging in heated debates that may damage your professional reputation.

Combining In-Person and Online Networking Communication:

1. Bridge the gap between in-person and online interactions: After meeting someone in person, connect with them on relevant online platforms to continue building the relationship. Follow up with a personalised message that references your conversation or their work. Engaging both in person and online allows you to maintain regular contact and stay top of mind with your connections.

2. Attend events and conferences with a social media presence: When attending networking events or conferences, use social media to your advantage. Share highlights, insights, or learnings from the event on your preferred platforms. Utilise event hashtags and tag relevant speakers or attendees to contribute to the online conversation and make connections with others who attended the event.

Effective networking communication is essential for building strong professional connections both in person and online. By mastering the art of communication, you can create memorable interactions, showcase your expertise, and cultivate meaningful relationships that can contribute to your long-term career success.

8.4 Networking for Diversity and Inclusion

In today's diverse and interconnected world, networking for diversity and inclusion has become increasingly important. Embracing diversity and creating inclusive networks can lead to a myriad of benefits, including access to new perspectives, enhanced creativity, improved problem-solving, and increased opportunities for personal and professional growth. In this section, we will explore the significance of networking for diversity and inclusion and strategies for fostering diverse networks.

Understanding the Importance of Diversity and Inclusion in Networking:

1. Broadening perspectives: By connecting with individuals from different backgrounds, cultures, and experiences, you gain access to a broader range of perspectives. This can challenge your own assumptions, expand your understanding of the world, and spark creativity.

2. Fostering innovation: Diverse networks encourage innovation and creativity by bringing together individuals with unique ideas and viewpoints. By embracing diversity and including

diverse voices in your network, you can enhance problem-solving, generate new ideas, and promote innovation within your industry or field.

3. Expanding opportunities: Creating diverse networks can open doors to new opportunities. By connecting with individuals who possess different skill sets, knowledge, and networks, you increase your chances of accessing a wider range of opportunities, such as job openings, collaborations, and partnerships.

Strategies for Fostering Diversity and Inclusion within Your Network:
1. Attend diverse networking events: Seek out networking events that specifically aim to foster diversity and inclusion. These events often bring together professionals from diverse backgrounds and industries, providing valuable opportunities to connect with individuals who may have different perspectives and experiences.

2. Be intentional in your outreach: Actively seek out individuals from underrepresented groups and make an effort to connect with them. Attend conferences, workshops, or meetups that cater to diverse communities and engage in conversations that promote inclusiveness. By actively seeking out

diverse individuals, you can expand your network and learn from their unique experiences.

3. Promote diversity within your existing network: Encourage diversity within your own network by introducing individuals from underrepresented groups to others in your network who may be in a position to provide opportunities or support. Act as a bridge, connecting individuals who can benefit from each other's expertise and experiences.

4. Create an inclusive environment: Foster an inclusive environment within your network by actively celebrating and valuing different perspectives, experiences, and contributions. Ensure that all members of your network feel welcome, respected, and included. Actively listen to diverse voices, give them ample opportunities to speak and share their ideas, and provide a platform for their voices to be heard.

5. Seek out mentors and advisors from diverse backgrounds: Cultivate relationships with mentors and advisors who possess diverse backgrounds and experiences. By seeking guidance from individuals who have faced unique challenges and triumphs, you can gain invaluable insights and perspectives that can enhance your personal and professional growth.

6. Embrace allyship: Act as an ally for individuals from underrepresented groups by actively supporting and advocating for their inclusion and representation within your network and broader professional community. Use your privilege and influence to amplify their voices and work towards creating a more inclusive environment for all.

By actively fostering diversity and inclusion within your network, you create an environment where all individuals can thrive, collaborate, and succeed. Embracing diversity not only cultivates a richer and more dynamic professional network but also contributes to a more equitable and inclusive society as a whole. Through networking for diversity and inclusion, we can collectively shape a future that embraces the value of all individuals, regardless of their background or identity.

CHAPTER 9

Harnessing the Power of Networking for Success

Networking has long been recognized as a powerful tool for achieving success in both personal and professional endeavours. By building meaningful connections and nurturing relationships, individuals can tap into a vast pool of resources, opportunities, and support. In this section, we will delve into the various ways in which networking can be harnessed for success and explore strategies for maximising its potential.

Using Your Network to Access Opportunities:
One of the primary benefits of networking is gaining access to a wide range of opportunities. By cultivating a strong and diverse network, you increase your chances of being exposed to new job openings, career advancements, business ventures, and collaborations. Your network can serve as a valuable source of information, providing insights into upcoming events, industry trends, and potential leads. Leveraging your network can help you stay ahead of the curve and open doors to new possibilities.

Leveraging Referrals and Recommendations:
A strong network can provide you with referrals and recommendations, which are powerful endorsements in today's competitive landscape. When seeking new job opportunities or business partnerships, having someone vouch for your skills and abilities can significantly increase your chances of success. Through networking, you can build relationships with professionals who are familiar with your work and can confidently recommend you to others. Referrals and recommendations carry a level of trust and credibility that can set you apart from other candidates or potential collaborators.

Building a Reputation as a Connector and Influencer:
Networking not only benefits you personally but also allows you to make a positive impact on others. By actively connecting individuals within your network and facilitating collaborations, you establish yourself as a valuable connector. This reputation can lead to increased visibility and influence within your industry or community. Becoming known as a trusted facilitator of opportunities and a resourceful problem-solver can enhance your professional brand and create a ripple effect of goodwill, ultimately leading to new connections, partnerships, and future success.

Maintaining and Sustaining Professional Relationships:

Building a network is not a one-time effort but an ongoing process that requires nurturing and maintenance. To harness the power of networking for long-term success, it is essential to invest time and effort in staying connected with your contacts. Regularly reach out to individuals in your network, provide support when needed, and celebrate their achievements. By building and maintaining meaningful relationships, you foster reciprocity and goodwill, increasing the likelihood that others will reciprocate the support and contribute to your success down the line.

Embracing Lifelong Learning and Continuous Networking:

Networking is not limited to specific moments or events – it is a continuous process that should be embraced throughout your professional journey. Actively seek out opportunities for continuous learning and development within your industry or field. Attend conferences, workshops, and seminars to stay updated on emerging trends, expand your knowledge base, and connect with like-minded professionals. By staying engaged and open to growth, you position yourself as a lifelong learner, which can lead to increased opportunities and success.

Expanding and Diversifying Your Network:

While it is crucial to maintain existing relationships, it is equally important to continuously expand and diversify your network. Seek out connections beyond your immediate circles, whether through attending industry-specific events, joining professional organisations, or engaging with online communities. Embracing diversity in your network brings new perspectives, fresh ideas, and a broader range of opportunities. By actively seeking out individuals from different backgrounds, industries, and experiences, you enrich your network and open doors to previously untapped potential.

Paying It Forward: Becoming a Networking Mentor:

As you grow and achieve success through networking, it is essential to pay it forward by becoming a mentor to others. Share your expertise, provide guidance, and actively support those who are seeking to grow their networks and achieve success. By helping others navigate the world of networking and supporting their professional journeys, you contribute to building a stronger and more interconnected community. Mentoring also allows you to expand your own network as you connect with individuals who appreciate and benefit from your guidance and support.

Harnessing the power of networking is crucial for achieving success in today's interconnected world. By leveraging your network to access opportunities, utilising referrals and recommendations, building your reputation as a connector and influencer, maintaining and nurturing relationships, embracing continuous learning, diversifying your connections, and becoming a networking mentor, you can unlock the full potential of networking for personal and professional growth. Remember that networking is not just about what you can gain but also about what you can contribute to the success of others, creating a virtuous cycle that uplifts the entire network.

9.1 Using Your Network to Access Opportunities

Networking provides individuals with the valuable advantage of accessing a wide range of opportunities. By actively building and nurturing relationships within their network, individuals can tap into a network's resources, connections, and knowledge, opening doors to new job opportunities, career advancements, business ventures, and collaborations.

One of the most powerful aspects of networking is the ability to gain insights into upcoming events, industry trends, and potential leads. Being connected to professionals who are active in your field provides you with a pulse on what's happening and what opportunities might be available. For example, a fellow network member might inform you about an industry conference or trade show that could be beneficial for your business growth. By attending such events, you increase your exposure, expand your knowledge, and have the chance to network with potential clients or partners.

Moreover, networking can help you gain access to hidden job opportunities. Many job openings are not publicly advertised but rather filled through personal connections and recommendations. When you have a robust network, individuals within it can become your advocates and share job openings that you might not have otherwise known about. They can introduce you to key decision-makers or even recommend you directly to potential employers. These referrals and recommendations carry significant weight and can give you a competitive edge in the job market.

In addition to accessing job and business opportunities, networking allows you to tap into the knowledge and expertise of others. Within your network, there might be individuals who have already achieved the level of success you aspire to or possess valuable knowledge and skills. Through networking, you can connect with these individuals and learn from their experiences. They can share insights, offer advice, and mentor you as you navigate your own path to success. By leveraging the expertise of others, you can accelerate your own growth and increase your chances of achieving your goals.

Also, your network can be a source of support and collaboration. When faced with challenges or seeking partnerships, your network can provide guidance and offer solutions. They can provide you with feedback, connect you with resources, or collaborate with you on projects. Having a strong support system within your network not only boosts your confidence but also expands your capabilities and helps you overcome obstacles more effectively.

To fully harness the power of your network for accessing opportunities, it is essential to actively engage with your connections. Regularly communicate with individuals in your network, share updates about your professional endeavours, and express interest in their projects or initiatives. Show genuine curiosity and take an active interest in their work. This way, when opportunities arise, your network will consider you as a potential candidate or collaborator.

Networking is not just about using others to advance your own goals; it is about building mutually beneficial relationships. Be willing to offer support and assistance to others within your network, as this will foster reciprocity. By being a valuable resource and a trusted member of your network, others will be more likely to reciprocate and help you when the time comes.

Networking is a powerful tool for accessing a myriad of opportunities. By actively building and nurturing relationships, professionals can tap into their network's resources, connections, and knowledge. Networking provides access to hidden job opportunities, referrals, knowledge and expertise, and a supportive community. To fully leverage your network for success, actively engage with your connections, offer support and assistance, and foster mutually beneficial relationships. By doing so, you expand your opportunities and increase your chances of achieving your goals.

9.2 Leveraging Referrals and Recommendations

In the world of professional networking, referrals and recommendations hold immense value. Leveraging the power of referrals and recommendations can significantly enhance your chances of success. When someone in your network puts their reputation on the line and vouches for your skills and abilities, it not only builds credibility but also opens doors to new opportunities.

One of the most effective ways to leverage referrals and recommendations is by actively seeking them out. When you have built strong relationships within your network, it becomes easier to ask for referrals. Reach out to individuals in your network who are familiar with your work and ask if they would be willing to recommend you to their contacts. Make it easy for them by providing a clear understanding of what you are looking for and how their recommendation would help you. By being specific about the type of opportunities you seek, you increase the likelihood of receiving targeted referrals.

Additionally, it is important to reciprocate by providing referrals and recommendations to others within your network. When you recommend someone based on their skills and experiences, you contribute to their professional credibility and increase their chances of success. This reciprocity not only strengthens your relationships but also encourages others to do the same for you.

When leveraging referrals and recommendations, it is crucial to have a strong personal brand. Ensure that your brand accurately represents your skills, expertise, and achievements. This way, when someone recommends or refers you, it aligns with the image you have created for yourself. Invest time in building a powerful online presence through platforms such as LinkedIn, where others can easily access information about your professional background and accomplishments.

Building a reputation as a reliable connector and influencer can also amplify the impact of referrals and recommendations. Actively make introductions and connect people within your network who could benefit from each other. By facilitating valuable connections, you become known as a valuable resource and a strategic connector. This reputation not only enhances the perception of your network but also increases the likelihood of others wanting to refer or recommend you.

When you receive a referral or recommendation, make sure to follow up promptly and professionally. Express your gratitude to the person who made the referral and keep them informed about the outcome. This not only shows your appreciation but also maintains the rapport and strengthens the relationship.

In addition to seeking referrals and recommendations from individuals within your network, consider reaching out to mutual connections or acquaintances who may have connections in your target industries or companies. Utilise the power of second and third-degree connections to expand your reach and tap into new opportunities.

It is essential to remember that referrals and recommendations should be genuine and earned. Focus on building authentic connections and delivering exceptional work that merits endorsements. When others enthusiastically vouch for your abilities, the impact on your professional growth can be tremendous.

Referrals and recommendations are powerful tools for networking success. Actively seek out referrals from individuals within your network, and reciprocate by providing recommendations for others. Build a strong personal brand and reputation as a reliable connector and influencer. Follow up promptly and professionally when you receive a referral, and express your gratitude. Remember that referrals and recommendations should be genuine and earned through authentic connections and delivering exceptional work. When utilised effectively, referrals and recommendations can open doors to new opportunities and significantly boost your chances of success.

9.3 Building a Reputation as a Connector and Influencer

In the realm of professional networking, building a reputation as a connector and influencer can be a game-changer for your career. As a connector, you become known as someone who actively makes introductions and connects individuals within your network who could benefit from knowing each other. Being an influencer means that your opinions and recommendations hold weight and influence the decisions and actions of others. By cultivating these roles within your professional network, you can enhance your credibility and open doors to new opportunities.

To build a reputation as a connector, it is important to actively seek out opportunities to make introductions and facilitate connections. Pay attention to the needs and interests of the individuals within your network and be proactive in identifying potential synergies. When you come across individuals who could benefit from knowing each other, reach out to both parties and explain why you believe they should connect. Provide a clear and compelling reason for the introduction, highlighting the potential benefits for both individuals involved. This not only showcases your understanding of their needs but also demonstrates your willingness to assist and add value.

Additionally, leveraging social media platforms can greatly amplify your role as a connector. Share relevant and valuable content that can spark conversations and facilitate connections. Utilise platforms such as LinkedIn to introduce individuals through mutual connections and showcase their expertise. By actively engaging in conversations and promoting collaboration, you position yourself as a connector and attract like-minded professionals to your network.

Building a reputation as an influencer requires you to establish your expertise and actively engage in thought leadership. Share your insights and experiences through blog posts, articles, and speaking engagements. Demonstrate your knowledge and expertise in your field and become a trusted source of information for others. Engage in meaningful conversations and discussions, both online and offline, that showcase your understanding and perspective. By consistently delivering valuable content and insights, you position yourself as an influencer and increase the likelihood that others will seek your guidance and recommendations.

Maintaining a reputation as a connector and influencer requires ongoing effort and dedication. Regularly nurture your relationships within your network and continue to provide value to others. Actively seek opportunities to connect individuals, even if it may not benefit you directly. Share relevant articles, job opportunities, and industry updates with your network to demonstrate your commitment to their success. By consistently adding value and showcasing your expertise, you solidify your reputation as a connector and influencer.

Building a reputation as a connector and influencer not only enhances your professional credibility but also expands your network and opens doors to new opportunities. As you connect individuals and share your insights, you become a valuable resource that others turn to for guidance and recommendations. This can lead to collaborations, partnerships, and career advancements that may not have been possible otherwise.

Building a reputation as a connector and influencer within your professional network can significantly enhance your career. Actively seek opportunities to connect individuals and showcase your expertise. Utilise social media platforms to amplify your role as a connector. Share valuable content and engage in thought leadership to position yourself as an influencer. Maintain your reputation by consistently adding value to others and nurturing your relationships. By cultivating these roles, you can strengthen your network, attract new opportunities, and ultimately achieve greater professional success.

CHAPTER 10

Networking for Long-Term Success

Networking is not just about short-term gains or immediate career opportunities. It is a strategic tool that, when utilised effectively, can lead to long-term success in your professional life. Building and nurturing relationships over time can create a strong foundation for personal and career growth. Here are some key strategies for networking for long-term success.

1. Maintain and Sustain Professional Relationships: One of the critical aspects of networking for long-term success is to maintain and sustain the relationships you build. Regularly staying in touch with your contacts, whether through emails, phone calls, or meetings, showcases your commitment to the relationship. Remember to show genuine interest in their lives and careers, celebrate their achievements, and provide support whenever they need it. By staying connected, you can continue to nurture these relationships and leverage them for future opportunities.

2. Embrace Lifelong Learning and Continuous Networking: The professional world is constantly evolving, and it is essential to stay up to date with industry trends, advancements, and new opportunities. Embrace lifelong learning by attending conferences, workshops, and seminars relevant to your field. Engage in continuous networking by actively seeking new connections and staying open to building relationships with individuals who can offer fresh perspectives and insights. By continually expanding your network and knowledge base, you position yourself as a valuable resource in your industry.

3. Expand and Diversify Your Network: While it's important to maintain existing relationships, expanding and diversifying your network is equally crucial for long-term success. Seek out individuals from diverse backgrounds, industries, and expertise areas. Engage in networking events and platforms that allow you to meet professionals outside your immediate circle. By connecting with a wide range of individuals, you expose yourself to different perspectives, opportunities, and potential collaborations. Diversifying your network can also provide a broader support system and increase your chances of tapping into new resources.

4. Pay It Forward: Becoming a Networking Mentor: As you progress in your career and build a strong network, don't forget the power of paying it forward. Act as a networking mentor to others who are starting their professional journeys or looking to expand their networks. Share your knowledge, experiences, and connections with them, and guide them in their own networking endeavours. By helping others succeed, you not only build goodwill but also strengthen your own network by establishing yourself as a valuable and trusted resource.

5. Foster a Supportive Network for Personal and Professional Growth: Networking should not only be about personal gain or career advancement. It should be a two-way street where you provide support and share resources with others, and they do the same for you. Foster a supportive network by actively engaging in collaborations, partnerships, and mentorship opportunities. Create a community of professionals who are invested in each other's growth and success. This supportive network can provide valuable advice, guidance, and opportunities throughout your career, contributing to your long-term success.

Networking for long-term success requires a strategic and proactive approach. Invest in maintaining and sustaining professional relationships, embrace lifelong learning, and continuously expand and diversify your network. Pay it forward by becoming a networking mentor, and foster a supportive network for both personal and professional growth. By utilising these strategies, you will create a strong foundation that will support your long-term success in your chosen field. Remember, networking is not a one-time event but an ongoing process that can lead to lifelong benefits.

10.1 Maintaining and Sustaining Professional Relationships

Building a strong professional network is not just about making new connections but also about maintaining and sustaining those relationships over time. This section will explore the importance of maintaining professional relationships and provide strategies for effectively nurturing and sustaining these connections.

Maintaining professional relationships is crucial because it allows you to stay connected with individuals who can provide valuable support, advice, and opportunities throughout your career.

These relationships can act as a source of mentorship, guidance, and even potential collaborations. By keeping these connections alive, you ensure a continuous flow of information, support, and opportunities.

One of the key strategies for maintaining professional relationships is regular communication. This includes staying in touch with your contacts, even if it's just a quick email or phone call to check in and see how they're doing. By showing genuine interest in their lives and careers, you build stronger connections and foster long-term relationships.

Additionally, attending networking events and industry conferences is an excellent way to reconnect with your professional network. These events provide valuable networking opportunities and allow you to establish face-to-face interactions with your contacts. By making an effort to attend these events and catching up with your connections, you demonstrate that you value the relationship and are committed to its maintenance.

Another effective strategy is to offer support and assistance to your professional contacts whenever possible. By sharing valuable resources, providing recommendations, or connecting them with other individuals in your network, you position yourself as a valuable asset and demonstrate your commitment to their success. This reciprocity strengthens the relationship and encourages your contacts to offer assistance in return when needed.

Maintaining professional relationships also involves being proactive in your approach. Take the initiative to reach out to your connections, congratulate them on their achievements, or check in with them during important milestones. By demonstrating genuine interest and staying connected, you stay at the forefront of their minds, increasing the likelihood of future collaborations and opportunities.

Moreover, leveraging technology and social media platforms can greatly facilitate the maintenance of professional relationships. Utilise tools like LinkedIn to stay connected with your network, engage with their posts, and share relevant industry news or resources. These platforms provide an easy way to stay updated on your contacts' professional activities and enable you to initiate conversations and maintain meaningful connections.

Lastly, always remember to express gratitude and appreciation towards your professional contacts. A simple thank-you note or a heartfelt expression of appreciation goes a long way in strengthening relationships. By acknowledging the support and guidance you've received, you demonstrate respect and reinforce the mutual value you place on the relationship.

Maintaining and sustaining professional relationships is crucial for long-term success. By regularly communicating, attending networking events, offering support, being proactive, leveraging technology, and expressing gratitude, you can successfully maintain and nurture your professional network. Remember that these relationships are not just about what you can gain, but it's also about providing support, guidance, and opportunities to others. By investing in these relationships, you create a strong and supportive network that can significantly contribute to your personal and professional growth.

10.2 Embracing Lifelong Learning and Continuous Networking

In the rapidly evolving professional landscape, it is essential to embrace lifelong learning and continuous networking to stay ahead and achieve long-term success. This section explores the importance of ongoing education and networking throughout one's career and provides strategies for effectively embracing these practices.

Continuous learning is crucial because it allows professionals to keep up with industry trends, technological advancements, and changes in best practices. By staying informed and adapting to new developments, individuals can remain competitive in their field and seize opportunities for growth and advancement. Lifelong learning also helps professionals develop new skills, expand their knowledge base, and enhance their problem-solving abilities.

Networking, when combined with continuous learning, amplifies the benefits and opportunities available. Building a network of industry experts and thought leaders provides access to a wealth of knowledge and insights. Engaging in conversations, attending seminars, and participating in workshops or webinars helps professionals stay current and gain valuable perspectives. Additionally, networking enables individuals to learn from others' experiences and receive guidance and mentorship from those who have already achieved success in their respective fields.

To embrace lifelong learning and continuous networking effectively, professionals should cultivate a growth mindset. This mindset involves adopting a willingness to learn, being open to new ideas, and embracing challenges as opportunities for growth. By approaching their careers with curiosity and a thirst for knowledge, individuals can unlock their full potential and forge meaningful connections.

Continuous learning can be achieved through various methods, such as enrolling in courses, attending industry conferences, and participating in webinars or workshops. Taking advantage of professional development opportunities provided by employers or industry organisations is also beneficial. Additionally, seeking out mentors and advisors who can guide and challenge you on your learning journey can accelerate growth and provide valuable insights.

Networking in a continuous manner involves actively seeking opportunities to expand and diversify your network. This can include attending networking events, joining professional associations, and participating in industry forums or online groups. Engaging in conversations with new contacts and maintaining relationships with existing connections is essential. Additionally, leveraging social media platforms and online networking tools can help professionals connect with a wider audience, share insights, and learn from others.

To make the most out of continuous learning and networking, professionals should foster a collaborative mindset. This involves embracing the idea of shared knowledge and actively participating in knowledge-sharing opportunities. By contributing to industry discussions, sharing insights, and collaborating with others, professionals can position themselves as connectors and influencers, further enhancing their network and reputation.

Embracing lifelong learning and continuous networking requires individuals to take ownership of their personal and professional development. This means setting goals for learning, networking, and professional growth. Regularly assessing and evaluating progress towards these goals is crucial to ensure ongoing improvement and development.

Embracing lifelong learning and continuous networking is essential for long-term success in today's professional landscape. By cultivating a growth mindset, actively pursuing learning opportunities, diversifying and expanding one's network, and fostering a collaborative mindset, professionals can stay current, navigate industry changes, and unlock new opportunities for growth. Remember that learning and networking are ongoing processes that should be integrated into your career journey to achieve continuous personal and professional development.

10.3 Expanding and Diversifying Your Network

In the quest for long-term success, it is crucial to continuously expand and diversify your professional network. As the saying goes, "Your network is your net worth," and by actively seeking out new connections and fostering relationships with individuals from different backgrounds and industries, you can unlock a world of opportunities and insights. This section explores the importance of expanding and diversifying your network and provides strategies for doing so effectively.

Expanding your network involves actively seeking out new connections and opportunities to meet professionals from various industries, disciplines, and backgrounds. By widening your circle, you expose yourself to fresh perspectives, new ideas, and potential collaborations. These diverse connections can provide valuable insights, challenge your thinking, and open doors to exciting opportunities.

One way to expand your network is by attending networking events and conferences. These gatherings provide a platform to meet professionals with similar interests or expertise, fostering valuable connections. Additionally, participating in industry-specific seminars, workshops, and panel discussions can introduce you to thought leaders and experts in your field. Taking advantage of these opportunities to engage in meaningful conversations and build relationships is crucial.

Another effective way to expand your network is by leveraging social media and online platforms. Joining professional groups and forums on platforms like LinkedIn can expose you to a global community of professionals. Actively participating in discussions, sharing insights, and connecting with individuals who share your interests or work in complementary fields can broaden your network exponentially. Additionally, engaging with online communities specific to your industry can provide access to a wealth of knowledge and collaboration opportunities.

Diversifying your network involves consciously seeking connections with individuals from different industries, backgrounds, and perspectives. When you limit yourself to networking within your immediate field, you may miss out on unique insights and innovative ideas.

To diversify your network, consider attending events and conferences outside of your industry or profession. Explore networking opportunities in fields that align with your interests or that offer a fresh perspective. Engaging with individuals from different backgrounds can help you think more creatively and approach challenges from new angles.

Additionally, joining professional associations and organisations that include individuals from diverse industries and backgrounds can provide opportunities for cross-industry networking. Engaging with people who work in different fields can spark innovation and provide access to resources you may not have encountered otherwise.

To effectively expand and diversify your network, it's essential to approach networking with an open mind and genuine curiosity. Value diverse perspectives and seek out connections that challenge your thinking and broaden your horizons. Remember that networking is a two-way street, and by offering your own insights, expertise, and connections, you can enrich others' networks and build mutually beneficial relationships.

Regularly reviewing and assessing your network is also crucial to ensure you continue to expand and diversify. Take inventory of your connections and identify areas where you may have gaps or opportunities for growth. Seek out individuals who can offer unique perspectives or connections that complement your existing network.

Expanding and diversifying your network is vital for long-term success. By actively seeking out new connections, attending networking events, leveraging online platforms, and engaging with diverse professionals, you can unlock a wealth of opportunities and insights. Embrace a mindset of embracing different perspectives, and continuously review and assess your network to ensure its growth and relevance. Remember that your network is an invaluable asset that can fuel your professional growth and open doors to exciting possibilities.

10.4 Paying It Forward: Becoming a Networking Mentor

Networking is not just about building connections for personal gain; it is also about giving back and helping others succeed. Becoming a networking mentor is a powerful way to share your knowledge, experience, and connections with others, ultimately creating a ripple effect of success. This section explores the importance of becoming a networking mentor and provides strategies for effectively mentoring others.

As you progress in your career and build a strong professional network, you acquire valuable knowledge, insights, and connections. By becoming a networking mentor, you can leverage these resources to empower others and contribute to their success. Mentoring not only benefits the mentees but also enhances your own leadership and communication skills, expands your network, and creates a legacy of impact.

One of the first steps in becoming a networking mentor is to identify individuals who could benefit from your guidance and support. Look for mentees who show potential, motivation, and a willingness to learn. These could be colleagues, junior professionals in your field, or individuals looking to transition into your industry.

Approach potential mentees with a genuine desire to help and guide them. Share your own experiences, successes, and challenges and listen actively to their goals and aspirations. Provide them with advice, feedback, and connections that can help them navigate their careers more effectively.

Networking mentors also play a critical role in building mentees' confidence and empowering them to take risks. Encourage mentees to step out of their comfort zones, attend networking events, and introduce themselves to new connections. Help them develop their personal brand and refine their communication and networking skills.

As a networking mentor, it is important to lead by example. Demonstrate the value of building strong professional relationships, attending networking events, and continuously learning. By showing mentees how networking has benefited your own career, you inspire them to prioritise networking and leverage its power.

In addition to one-on-one mentoring, consider organising mentorship programs or networking events within your organisation or industry. These initiatives provide a platform for mentees to connect with multiple mentors and gain diverse perspectives. By facilitating these programs, you create a supportive networking community that nurtures professional growth and development.

It's worth noting that mentoring is a two-way street. While you are sharing your knowledge and expertise, be open to learning from your mentees as well. They may have fresh insights, perspectives, or connections that can benefit you. Embrace the opportunity to grow and expand your own network through these mentoring relationships.

Furthermore, mentorship is not limited to formal arrangements. Sometimes, even a casual conversation or a simple introduction can have a profound impact on someone's career. Consider how you can integrate mentoring into your everyday interactions and make a positive difference in someone's professional journey.

Becoming a networking mentor is a powerful way to give back and help others succeed. By sharing your knowledge, experiences, and connections, you can empower mentees and contribute to their growth and development. Take the initiative to identify potential mentees, offer guidance and support, and lead by example. Mentoring is a mutually beneficial relationship that enhances your own skills and expands your network. Embrace this opportunity to make a lasting impact and create a network of success that extends far beyond your own reach.

CONCLUSION

As we come to the end of "Professional Networking: Building Connections for Success," it is our hope that this comprehensive guide has provided you with the essential tools, strategies, and mindset necessary to revolutionise your professional networking skills.

Networking is not merely a means to an end—it is a transformative journey that opens doors to countless opportunities, invaluable relationships, and continuous growth. By embracing the power of networking, you are setting yourself up for success in ways you may have never imagined.

Throughout this book, we explored the importance of cultivating a networking mindset and setting clear goals. We dived into practical strategies for building and maintaining a professional network, as well as specialised techniques tailored to specific contexts. We addressed the challenges and obstacles that may arise, and provided you with the skills to overcome them. From effective conversation techniques to networking etiquette and best practices, we equipped you with the knowledge needed to thrive in any networking situation.

But our journey does not end here. Networking is an ongoing process, and as you forge ahead, we encourage you to continually nurture and expand your network. Challenge yourself to step out of your comfort zone, engage in meaningful conversations, and seek out new perspectives. Remember that networking is not just about what others can do for you, but also about how you can contribute to the success of others.

Throughout your professional journey, leverage your network to access opportunities, find mentors and advisors, and build collaborative partnerships. Embrace the role of a connector and influencer, using your position to uplift others and foster a supportive network. Most importantly, strive to create an inclusive and diverse network that celebrates equality and promotes innovation.

As you embark on this networking adventure, keep in mind that success lies not only in the number of connections you establish but also in the quality of those relationships. Be authentic, genuine, and generous in your interactions. Cherish each connection as a unique opportunity to learn, grow, and make a positive impact.

Now, armed with the knowledge and strategies shared in this book, it is time to take your networking journey to new heights. Embrace the power of building connections, strive for excellence in your interactions, and watch as your professional life unfolds with newfound opportunities and achievements.

Remember, you have the power to shape your destiny through the connections you forge. Network confidently, network purposefully, and network with passion. The world is waiting for the impact you will make through your powerful professional network. Let the journey begin!